"*Calling the Church out of Egypt* is challenging and will leave you questioning, not who you are or whose you are, but rather if you've been living your life with chains weighing you down. As someone who has seen first-hand the life of Jo McGuffin lived out, I can assure you the words you read in the Bible can and should be still lived out today. Healing, freedom, and transformation are not just stories of old, but rather everyday life for now. This book brought me back to the basics, to simply focus on God and WHO He is. My 'self' will take care of itself, as I keep my eyes on Him. Love you, Mom."
—*Jordan McGuffin, Missionary & Fitness Coach*

"I have known Jo McGuffin for eighteen years. God has used her greatly, and she has a heavy anointing on her. We have been each other's armor bearer for many years. Jo is not only an excellent nurse, but a qualified teacher, and her preaching is outstanding. Jo has touched many people through salvation, healing, and deliverance. She is deeply used in the prophetic and co-founded the Zoe Healing Center, an international organization for ministries of healing, restoration, and equipping whole families. Jo hears from the Lord and if He says so, she won't back away from anything! She is a good leader.

"The words of 'out of Egypt' were given to Jo from the Lord. The Lord then began to lead her into the organization of a book. She was somewhat shocked! For those He uses prophetically to pen works of thoughts and ideas, they will understand how this process works, as I do.

"*Calling the Church out of Egypt* is a great read. God is still today trying to lead people out of Egypt. God had brought them out and placed the knowledge of His desires through His Word in the churches, but man began dealing with the spirits of Satan. Now, we are right back today, needing redemption: giving up our lives and receiving God and living totally in Him. The Lord is wooing! For those who will, God is using people to awaken His Spirit in their hearts and bring them into a spiritual understanding of salvation, healing, and deliverance.

"Pick up this book today and let it open your understanding to the deeper things of God. You will never be the same; on this you can rely. This is very clear, very precise information about where we have been and if we make our hearts right, where we should be going! All scriptures are right on. Deeply dedicated Christians who read this book (and scriptures) will shiver as the Holy Spirit flow will fill their being! His Presence will fill their hearts."

—*Sharon Warn Decker, Intercessory and Prophetic Prayer Minister; Author,* For Such a Time as This

"Jo McGuffin's book is right on time. *Calling the Church out of Egypt* has been decades in the making. Through personal experience of God's supernatural healing, Jo thrust herself into the health care profession. From ICU Nurse to hospital administrator, she has seen much of the best of what man has to offer. She has seen how the Church has surrendered the need for healing—physical, emotional and spiritual—to the Health Care system. Although God has blessed humanity with the wonders of scientific breakthrough in medicine, she has experienced that God is the Great Physician. Jo has witnessed where God has been sidelined in health care; worldly practices have crept into our way of thinking. Having witnessed firsthand the supernatural power of God to heal all our infirmities, she helps the Church to once again focus on the Great I Am and for us to believe in the healing power of God that comes through His Son Jesus Christ!"

—*Tom Donnan, Intercessory and Prophetic Prayer Minister; Author,* Healing the Nation; *Healing the Nation Ministries*

"*Calling the Church Out of Egypt* is a powerful journey through Scripture that will challenge and transform your thinking and understanding of what God is really saying throughout His Word that is absolutely relevant and necessary for today's believers who are trying to be godly in an ungodly culture. Jo is a respected teacher, leader, medical professional, and author who lives out daily what she says and has a deep revelation that God is who He says He is and does what He says He'll do. It has been an

honor and a privilege to learn from Jo, a woman of integrity and character who loves God and people wholeheartedly. If you desire to know and serve God in a radical way, and to know that you never have to settle for less than God's best, I urge you to read this book. It will transform your life!"
—*Amber Guthery, Executive Director of Operations, Zoe Healing Center*

"A fearless and unpretentious woman of God has written a book that is so informative and full of truth you won't be able to put it down. It is time to embrace the truth of God's Word and stop believing lies."
—*Reverend Rebecca A. LaFleur, Evangelist; Breaking Chains Ministry*

"Jo McGuffin reveals the misconception that most people have embraced in an attempt for physical and emotional healing. She also brings the reader to Light, the true path for complete wholeness through Jesus Christ."
—*Pastor Phil Corbett, Author, Evangelist, Second Wind Ministries*

"Jo McGuffin is a gift to the kingdom. Her accessible way of breaking down Kingdom principles to bring freedom has been invaluable to the success of our ministry in the lives of dozens of students. Jo does it all with a humble heart, equipping the church and giving all glory to Jesus."
—*Reverend Cynthia Dobbs, Author; Co-Pastor, Chi Alpha Student Ministries, Oklahoma State University*

Calling the Church out of Egypt

You Have Been Delivered: Jesus Is Alive
Live Loved; Live Well; Live Him!

Jo McGuffin

Mobile, Alabama

Calling the Church out of Egypt by Jo McGuffin
Copyright © 2018 Jo McGuffin
All rights reserved under the copyright laws of the United States of America. This material may not be copied or reprinted for commercial gain or profit. The use of short quotations or occasional page copying for personal or group study is permitted and encouraged. Permission will be granted upon request.

Unless otherwise stated, all Scripture quotations are taken from The Holy Bible, English Standard Version, copyright ©2001 by Crossway, a publishing ministry of Good News Publishers. Used by permission. All rights reserved.

Scripture quotations marked NKJV are taken from the New King James Version. Copyright ©1982 by Thomas Nelson. Used by permission. All rights reserved.

Scripture quotations marked HCSB are taken from the Holman Christian Standard Bible. Copyright ©2009 by Holman Bible Publishers, Nashville Tennessee.

Scripture quotations marked AMP are taken from the Amplified Bible. Copyright © 2015 by the Lockman Foundation, La Habra, CA. Used by permission. All rights reserved.

Scripture quotations marked TLB are taken from The Living Bible by Kenneth N. Taylor, Used by permission of Tyndale House, Wheaton, IL. All are used by permission. All rights reserved.

Scripture quotations marked NASB are taken from the *New American Standard Bible*, Copyright ©1960, 1962, 1963, 1968, 1971, 1973, 1975, 1977 by The Lockman Foundation.

Scripture quotations marked KJV are taken the King James version of the Bible. In public domain.

ISBN 978-1-58169-700-1
For Worldwide Distribution
Printed in the U.S.A.

Gazelle Press
P.O. Box 191540 • Mobile, AL 36619
800-367-8203

Note to the Reader

The book is designed to provide inspiration, information, and motivation for spiritual growth towards a relationship with God through Jesus Christ. The purpose is to acquaint the reader with what the Bible teaches: If you are sick or have problems, God wants to heal and set you free.

The views, information, or opinions expressed in the book are the author's personal philosophy and biblical worldview interpretation. It is not intended to reflect the views of a denomination, healthcare organization, publisher, or individual professional.

The book is not intended to give medical, psychological, or legal advice because it is not diagnosis or treatment focused, but God's Word and promises focused. Each person must make their own decision about their own soul; each person must also be solely responsible for their own health choices and decisions.

It is the author's prayer that the reader shall experience spiritual growth and physical blessings through the truths in God's Word. The author encourages each person to do their own research and verification, with any practice concerning health and wellness. References are provided for informational and educational purposes and with good faith, content and links were accurate at the time of access; however, websites, access, and content are subject to change. It is encouraged that each person seeking God, read the Bible for themselves, which the author believes is God's revealed will and ways. It is the sole responsibility of the reader to make their own informed decision as it relates to holistic health: body, soul, and spirit.

Contents

1 You Have Been Delivered. Wait, What? Is That True? *1*
2 But What Happened? Where Did We Get Sidetracked? *9*
3 Trust and Obey—God Means What He Said *14*
4 History of Medicine and Psychology *20*
5 Spiritual Psychology: Your Invitation to the Occult *32*
6 Heart Intelligence *56*
7 Pharaoh Has Been Challenged: Are You Desperate Yet? *90*
8 God's Redemptive Plan Includes Healing and Provision *167*
9 Calling All Full Gospel Believers *178*
10 The Final Hour Is Here: A Prophetic Warning *182*
11 Inspecting Your Foundation *209*

Introduction

It is impossible to pray with faith if you don't know the will of God. It is hard to truly trust someone you don't really know. Could it be the things you perceive that you are in spiritual warfare against, in reality—is God warring against the very things you are pursuing? Could it be that you are blindly giving the devil a platform and pursuing the kingdom of darkness? Could it be that your source of truth is the hindrance standing against the promises of God for your life?

I have academic credentials, but my credentials that matter are straight forward. I am in love with Jesus. I am a devoted Christ follower and a student of the Holy Scriptures. I am under the headship of Jesus Christ and under the influence and power of the Holy Spirit who is the greatest Counselor, Comforter, and Teacher of Truth. I am a child of God and I serve in His Kingdom through the priceless blood of Jesus.

The meaning of life is the wrong question to be pursuing. The question is who is your source of life? Our purpose as disciples is to reconcile people to God (2 Corinthians 5:18) and make more disciples (Matthew 28:19-20). In other words, know Jesus and make Him known. Let this be a time to let the Holy Spirit examine your heart—let the Holy Spirit speak to you for your lifestyle and situations. May you be encouraged because of God's steadfast mercy and love, but make the appropriate adjustments to line up with the Word of God which is the only standard for your soul. Then fill up with His Presence through the precious promise of the Holy Spirit.

Become a devoted, first century, follower of Christ that Jesus is calling in this hour. Let Him transform you by the renewing of your mind by the Word of God and in the knowledge of Him. Quit listening to the opinions and traditions of men, and let Jesus transform you into the person God created and redeemed you to be—complete in Him! Don't settle for less than God's best. He gave it all on the Cross so that I can live. There is no Plan B. There it is!

This is an urgent, end-time message, to those who profess to know Christ as well as for those who are struggling with their faith and belief in God. In addition, this message of warning is for those who are participating in or searching other philosophies, traditions, and spiritual pathways in an effort to find themselves or God.

You have already been delivered but you choose your source of life and future destiny. Live well and live loved!

> *The things which you learned and received and heard and saw in me, these do and the God of peace will be with you* (Philippians 4:9 NKJV).

Dedication Prayer

Father, God, I dedicate this to You. I believe that it was You that dropped this into my heart and gave me the words and the profound urgency to write this for such a time as this. Lord, thank You for loving us first; thank You for fashioning, directing, and establishing my steps in a journey to seek You and know You. Jesus, You are the Way, the Truth, and the Life, and no one comes to the Father any other way. Thank You for the privilege to make disciples, instructing them in Your Word and Your ways, and seeing people saved, healed, set free, and walking in the power and fullness of You, as You created and redeemed us to be. You are a good, good Father. Thank You, God, that You have not changed! You are the same yesterday, today, and forever.

Thank You, God, for my family—what precious beautiful gifts! When I dedicated my marriage, my husband, and my two precious children to You, I trusted that all would love You, obey You, and love Your truth, Your Word, and finally, to finish well when we meet You face to face.

I stand in awe of the things that You have done and are doing. Thank You that my family is grounded in Your word—the full gospel—and I see Your hand constantly upon them, establishing their steps to fulfill Your calling and purpose for their lives. Thank You, Lord, that even when I make people uncomfortable because of my passion for You and Your ways, I know that You are impacting lives around us.

Thank You, Lord, for the people in my life that have taught me, challenged me, and along with my family and Holy Spirit, keep me accountable to Your Word with my speech and my actions. Thank You for my amazing life experiences that have been validated by Your Word! Testimonies continue to speak of Your greatness and glory and encourage others to love and follow You.

I give You this material to do with what You choose, to go where You desire, and I trust that You will place it in the hands of those You have already purposed it to be. I trust You, God, the King of my heart!

—*Jo, Your Daughter, Disciple of Jesus*

For I know the plans I have for you, declares the Lord, plans for welfare and not for evil, to give you a future and a hope. Then you will call upon me and come and pray to me, and I will hear you. You will seek me and find me, when you seek me with all your heart.

                    Jeremiah 29:11-13

One

You Have Been Delivered. Wait, What? Is That True?

When Joshua was appointed, one of his many qualifications God highlighted was his faith. All through the wilderness journey we encounter people opposing God, stemming from change, unbelief and fear. The same today ... victorious voices are being met with opposition from people, just like Israel of old, "despise the pleasant land..." (Psalm 106:24). But praise God, once again, we see God raising up a people, who will lead and stop at nothing to fulfill His purposes and enter into their full inheritance and rest. Those they lead will be blessed and empowered to fulfill God's purposes as well! Challenges in life and to our well-being are opportunities for Him to reveal more of Himself as He leads, instructs, counsels, and changes us.

Psalms 106 and 107 describe God's people from the onset of their deliverance from Egypt. God had always had a redemptive plan from the very beginning. God's people, however, continued to sin—their sin was unbelief and doubt. They walked in unbelief that God would really take care of them. They soon forgot God's works and His abundant love towards them; they did not wait on His counsel, resulting in their worshipping foreign gods and adopting the ways of foreign cultures. They provoked God to jealousy, but even more so, they sorely grieved a Father who loved them so much. Every time, however, in the midst of their unbelief and unfaithfulness to Him, God's abundant love was steadfast.

God did not change! What changed is that there was a shift of expectation for the people of God just before Joshua led them across the Jordan River. This time, God gave them instructions to cleanse and consecrate themselves, and the priest had to get their feet wet first before they saw the miracle. Up until this time, they were used to God just doing everything for them. Now they had to believe, which meant acting upon what God said, before they saw the miracle. Can we believe today that God's plan for redemption was fulfilled in Jesus—He finished the work upon the Cross, was resurrected, and is now at the right hand of Father interceding for us? God expects us to believe Him, which also now requires that we act on what God says before we see the miracle.

"Faith is the substance of things hoped for, the evidence of things not seen" (Hebrews 11:1 NKJV). The *English Standard Version* uses the word "assurance" rather than "substance." Both words, in the original Greek, literally mean, "under something" as in a title or property deed—in other words, something guaranteed. *The Holman Bible* (HCSB) states it this way: "Now faith is the reality of what is hoped for, the proof of what is not seen."

We activate our faith by our actions. We receive salvation, healing, and deliverance by grace! Faith is our connector to God's grace. Faith is when we believe Jesus for who He is and what He says through His Word, and we should then act out what we believe. In other words, our actions speak to people what we believe and not our words.

Yes, I choose to believe that Jesus is all He says He is. I have chosen to trade my caduceus symbol for the Cross!

In Matthew 6:25-34 Jesus says to us:

Therefore I tell, do not be anxious about your life, what you will eat or what you will drink, nor about your body, what you will put on. Is not life more than food, and the body more than clothing? Look at the birds of the air: they neither sow nor reap nor gather into barns, and yet, your heavenly Father feeds them. Are you not of more value than they? And which of you by being anxious can add a single hour to his span of life? And why are you anxious ... O, you of little faith? Therefore do not be anxious, saying, "What shall we eat?" or "What shall we drink?" or "What shall we wear?" For the Gentiles seek after all these things, and your heavenly Father knows that you need them all. But seek first the Kingdom of God and His righteousness, and all these things will be added to you. Therefore do not be anxious for tomorrow, for tomorrow will be anxious for itself. Sufficient for the day is its own trouble.

In context of the whole Bible and counsel of God—God is saying that if you seek Him first, and know Him, He will back up His word with provision and power to fulfill His purposes and instructions given to us today. God **has not** changed from the beginning of time.

What Is God Saying Today? He Speaks Perfectly

Enter by the narrow gate. For the gate is wide and the way is easy that leads to destruction, and those who enter by it are many. For the gate is narrow and the way is hard that leads to life, and those who find it are few Beware of false prophets, who come to you in sheep's clothing but inwardly are ravenous wolves. You will recognize them by their fruits. Are grapes gathered from thorn bushes or figs from thistles? So every healthy tree bears good fruit, but the diseased tree bears bad fruit. A healthy tree cannot bear bad fruit, nor can a diseased tree bear good fruit. Every tree that does not bear good fruit is cut down and thrown into the fire. Thus you will recognize them by their fruits (Matthew 7:13-20).

In Matthew 7:21-23 Jesus speaks:

*"Not everyone who says to me 'Lord, Lord,' will enter the kingdom of heaven, **but the one who does the will of my Father** who is in heaven. On that day many will say to me 'Lord, Lord, did we not prophesy in your name, and cast our demons in your name, and do many mighty works in your name?' And then will I declare to them, 'I never knew you; depart from me, you workers of lawlessness."*

Matthew 7:24-27 warns us to build our house on the right foundation; *a solid foundation which is Jesus Christ and Him alone.* Jesus says,

"Everyone then who hears these words of mine and does them will be like a wise man who built his house on the rock. And everyone who hears these words of mine and does not do them will be like a foolish man who built his house on the sand. And the rain fell, and the floods came the winds blew and beat against that house, and it fell, and great was the fall of it."

Jesus, this Rock, spent three years, proclaiming the Kingdom of God is here. Throughout the Gospel recordings, Jesus went everywhere teaching as One who had authority, proclaiming the Kingdom, calming storms, healing the sick, casting out demons, and raising the dead! During that time, He also made His disciples into preaching, teaching, and healing teams. And praise God, He is still making disciples to go out into dark places, representing Him and sharing His message of redemption and healing to those who will believe so that they do not have to perish. Those that believe can live life with the fullness of God, testifying to the resurrection of Jesus and are able to accomplish what He purposed each of us to do on the earth. We can be saved, healed, set free, and living in the fullness of what God created us and redeemed us to be.

And to the centurion, Jesus said, "Go: let it be done for you as you have believed" (Matthew 7:13).

His servant who was paralyzed was healed.

That evening they brought to him many who were oppressed by demons, and he cast out spirits with a word and healed all who were sick. This was to fulfill what was spoken by the prophet, Isaiah: 'He took our illnesses and bore our diseases (Matthew 7:16-17).

Wait, What? Is That True?

A tragedy has occurred today because the lost and hurting do not see the manifestation of Jesus surrounding those that confess to be Christ followers. Not only does the world notice a stark difference between the New Testament disciples and the so called disciples today, those of us confessing to be in the Body of Christ are also noticing!

I have had Christ-following students from other countries come to the U.S. and ask me point blank, "Where are the churches that believe the Jesus of the Bible?" The Jesus that many are following is a hologram image or just another superhero with secret weaknesses, created on man's desires—without substance and power—not the Jesus, God's Son, of the Bible.

That problem has been burning in my heart and birthing in my mind for several years; and subsequently, through the Holy Spirit's instructions, I began a journey to transition out of traditional healthcare practice into being a first century Christ follower. I could see the growing dichotomy between what the world experts were offering and practicing, and what God said. Health and wellness practitioners, that include mental health professionals, are among the most compassionate, kind, and respected people I know, but they are only practicing within the scope of the knowledge that has been given them. One can have a loving attitude and show great compassion for people and yet still miss the mark with a desired outcome. Modern medicine and wellness alternatives that include spirituality and psychology all come from worldviews that are based on another foundation rather than Jesus. Humanism and other worldviews do not mix with the Holy Spirit—they are like oil and water.

We are deceived when we use the term Christian to secular disciplines, such as Christian psychologist or licensed counselor. The truth is you have a person, who confesses to be a Christian, attempting to incorporate biblical knowledge and principles into the practice of psychology or sociology, or whatever new "ology," promoting to restore peace, civility, a healthy body, or a sound mind.

Even in my own denomination, we have a counseling agency number listed on the back of a minister's ordination card, in case a minister personally needs help. I attempted to get the number and advertisement removed and placed in another venue for promotion, but was lovingly told from our national office that the counseling agency was founded by an ordained minister and was biblically sound. And no, it could not be removed from future cards. Do you see the deception—people think it is okay to call and promote psychology based experts instead of God alone? Later, I will address the origin and history of such humanistic world-view practices, and this deception will become more discerning.

There is no such thing as Christian psychology or Christian medicine from another worldview. A biblical Christian worldview is Christ and He alone. There are products and services from metaphysical (beyond the natural realm) or other New Age worldviews, along with humanism infiltrating the churches. Energy healing is one example of such alternative healing modality. One type even claims to produce healing of the mind, body, and offers spiritual enlightenment through oils and other therapies that are promoted to contain a life force energy. Their training website entices believers to "come learn the art of healing like Jesus did." In the literature and manual, they describe not only how to do a healing service in a church, but use actual scriptures to convince the practitioners and participants that this lines up with the whole counsel of God, but it doesn't! Many alternative medicines and therapies are packaged with occult practices taught by both health care and "spiritual" professionals, such as Therapeutic Touch and Reiki, to name just two. Listen to the Holy Spirit and ask Him to lead you into Truth.

People are perishing, cancer is rampant, and suicide is now epidemic in the body of Christ! Those that profess to know Christ are experiencing horrendous side effects from toxins labelled medicine or an alternative; people are overweight, depressed, with mental health issues, and dying prematurely from suicide, invasive medical treatments, and drugs. Does that sound like compassion or best practice? Does it sound like the best interests of a good Father? Does this sound like the majesty and goodness of God? It is not.

Choose Life

Our walk with God is an individual relationship with Him; however, I choose to trust that the most excellent way—the only way—to trust and know the God of Abraham, my God, is through knowing His Son, Jesus, and Him alone!

I choose Life—the person of Jesus Christ—who bore my sickness and disease and paid my penalty of death so that I could live healthy and free from bondage here on earth to fulfill His purpose given to me and then forever be with Him in eternity. Now that is a good, good Father! That is God's medicine! Do you really know Him?

For they [His words] *are life to those who find them, and healing to all their flesh* (Proverbs 4:22).

What is your source of health and wellness? Peace and restfulness? Provision? To whom are you listening? From whom are you getting counsel and advice? From man's opinion and wisdom or God? From created images—other gods or products—or God's Word?

Oppression is anything hindering you from being all that you were created and redeemed to be. Sickness, pain, depression, and even poverty are all oppressors; we desperately try to eliminate them at all costs, and if we can't, we numb ourselves or give up. The issues become—what is your source of life? What are you willing to put up with and keep tolerating? And from whom do you believe for your salvation, healing, and deliverance? Whatever the issue or question is, the answer, for the Christ follower, is always the same—Jesus!

I am the door, if anyone enters by me, he will be saved and will go in and out and find pasture. The thief comes only to steal and kill and destroy. I came that they may have life and have it abundantly. I am the good shepherd. The good shepherd lays down his life for the sheep (John 10:9-10).

He himself bore our sins in his body on the tree, that we might die to sin and live to righteousness. By his wounds you have been healed. For you were straying like sheep, but have now returned to the Shepherd and overseer of your souls (1 Peter 2:24-25).

The sorrows of those who run after another god will multiply; their drink offerings of blood I will not pour out or take their names on my lips. The Lord is my chosen portion and my cup; you hold my lot. The lines have fallen for me in pleasant places; indeed, I have a beautiful inheritance (Psalm 16:4-6).

My son, do not forget my teaching, but let your heart keep my commandments, for length of days and years of life and peace they will add to you. Let not steadfast love and faithfulness forsake you; bind them around your neck; write them on the tablet of your heart.

In all your ways acknowledge him, he will make straight your paths. Be not wise in your own eyes; fear the Lord and turn away from evil. It will be healing to your flesh and refreshment to your bones.

My son, do not lose sight of these—keep sound wisdom and discretion, and they will be life for your soul and adornment for your neck. Then you will walk on your way securely and your foot will not stumble. If you lie down, you will not be afraid; when you lie down, your sleep will be sweet (Proverbs 3:1-2, 6-8, 21-24).

My son, be attentive to my words; incline your ear to my sayings. Let them not escape from your sight; keep them within your heart. For they are life to those who find them and healing to all their flesh (Proverbs 4:20-22).

Two

But What Happened? Where Did We Get Sidetracked?

When did we get sidetracked so that the Gospel is no longer as recognizable or credible today, specifically in the West? God purposed us to still be those people turning the world upside down. Jesus purchased our salvation, our liberty, and our healing. Freedom is not the absence of something (bondage), but the presence of Someone—Jesus. Free people free people!

God Had a Plan

God had a plan—every contingency was planned. With the birth of Moses, God had plans for him to lead His people out of Egypt into freedom. As they left, God continually made provision for them. He placed a cloud covering over the camp during the day, and at night He provided heat and light by His hand. He knew where the water was and how and what they would eat. God had things planned, but He also knew that His people would be tried and tested. *Faith has never been built on situational miracles but rather a lifestyle of relationship.*

God's people saw mighty miracles but ended up without faith. God had promises but took the people to the wilderness for a place of testing because He loved the world as He still does now. God was trying to raise up a people with a testimony—a people that could go out as witnesses of His nature of truth and goodness. The same is for His people today—God didn't save us so we could just receive His grace, goodness, and mercy for ourselves. He is looking for people who are not talking and teaching an unproven gospel. He is equipping people that are *tried, tested, and prove Him faithful* and who actually believe the gospel that is preached. I believe God expects us to trust and believe Him without doubting, even in the most impossible situations. Without faith, it is impossible to please Him.

We tell the world who Jesus is—our Savior, our Healer, our Deliverer. We tell the world that God can do the impossible. We then get into distress, trials, and even impossible situations, we fall apart, grasping at anyone and anything that gives us a glimpse of hope or a promise of a cure. Well, the world is watching! An example of this is when King Darius actually believed what Daniel said about his God. God didn't save Daniel *from* the lions' den, He saved him *in* the lion's den. Daniel trusted God "before the sons of man." King Darius made a decree for his entire country, "that men tremble and fear before the God of Daniel for He is the Living God and steadfast forever… He delivers and rescues and works signs and wonders in heaven and earth" (Daniel 6:26). People listen to what is said by the actions that demonstrate what we believe.

> *Oh how great is Thy goodness which Thou has laid up for them that fear Thee; which Thou hast wrought for them that trust in Thee before the sons of man* (Psalm 31:19 KJV).

Goodness can be portrayed many ways, but to a follower of Christ still on the earth, that goodness is a testimony of God's glory! Daniel had a testimony. Daniel believed what he preached. King Darius believed because he witnessed Daniel place his trust in His God. He witnessed Daniel prove that God was trustworthy.

A Testimony Requires a Test

God's desire is for all of His children to come to a place where we can face any situation or trial or obstacle without falling apart, without looking to other sources and solutions, and people. God's desire is a total confidence and dependence upon Him. This place is the place of rest that God still offers His children today, but few find Him.

The rest is a promise—it's something you can't work up with your emotions or positive thinking or the right worship environment. One must lay down your own life and efforts and totally embrace Truth—a person, Jesus Christ. It is a divine rest that comes from the Holy Spirit to those who believe God with childlike faith. It is a trust that demonstrates complete confidence in the Lord and that He does all things well.

Testimony

In one of our home small group meetings, I asked for prayer requests like we always do. This particular week, one of our 10-year-old students asked for prayer for a spider bite on her leg. She was experiencing pain, swelling, and fever. With her family and the entire group observing, I knelt to lay my hand on her leg to pray for her.

The Lord asked me to ask her this question: "If tonight before you went to sleep, your dad told you he would be back to kiss you good night, would you believe him?"

She said, "Yes."

I asked her, "Why?"

She burst out without hesitation, "Because my Dad always does what he says he will do!"

It was a beautiful picture, because then I explained to her that God is a wonderful Father to all of us who love Him as well, and He will always do what He says He will do. I prayed a simple prayer in agreement with what God already said, in 1 Peter 2:24. "He Himself bore our sins in His body on the tree, that we might die to sin and live to righteousness. By His wounds you have been healed."

She went home with her family shortly afterwards. Later that evening, her mom called and said they noticed on the way home that the pain and fever were gone. When her mom was getting ready to dress the wound before bed, the black pus part popped out and fell on the floor.

We thanked the Lord that He is our Healer. She sent me a picture the next day and the wound was so faded, one could hardly notice that there had been a mark. Child-like faith!

Confidence—childlike faith—is entering into God's rest that He will do what He says He will do. It is an absolute trust that God's love towards me is absolute and a loving Father would never hurt one of His children. It would be cruel and disgusting for Him to see a child hurt, in agony or pain, and just stand by not entering their pain and suffering, and not do everything in His power to save, heal, and deliver. God did do everything in His power—He sent His only Son to die. If there was any other way, I believe God would have told us and He certainly would have spared His Son. No words can describe that kind of love. I believe God expects us to love others like He loves us; however, it is impossible to do so without His power being demonstrated through us as well. The world is watching!

TESTIMONY

Over 20 years ago, I began experiencing acute symptoms of pancreatitis. It began with pain in my left side and abdomen. I would suddenly become nauseated, tingly, and almost black-out. I would immediately have to hold on to something and drop to the floor. The episodes became more frequent. The doctor reported from a scan that my pancreas was irregular and was working me up for pancreatitis. No, this could not continue. I had grade-school children. I was a full-time professor of nursing at the local university. My husband was a military officer with multiple important responsibilities and was often out of pocket for training exercises. I had ministry responsibilities at church each week. I taught STARS—a young girls' ministry small group.

I had already had a relationship with God and had experienced mighty miracles in my life and believed in divine healing. I prayed, thanking God for His Word and sending His Son for me, and declared my healing in Jesus' name. As I kept thanking Him, my pain disappeared. I testified in front of my church the next Sunday. I never went back for a follow-up—I didn't need confirmation as a sign. I just believed. As of today, I have never had any further symptoms.

Childlike faith. My Father said it, and He always does what He says.

Three

Trust and Obey— God Means What He Said

God is clear in His instructions or commandments to those that choose to follow Him, both in the old and new covenants. It is interesting to note that many people perceive God's commandments as being no longer relevant or as coming from a legalistic, restrictive viewpoint. What is so amazing to me is that God gave His first commandments to people with whom He already had a relationship! God shows us His *goodness* by placing spiritual boundaries around us for *protection* from His *wisdom* as a loving good Father/child relationship. From my relationship with God, even when I don't fully understand Him, I can trust Him to know best from His point of view as He counsels, guides, sometimes redirects, and comforts me.

People seem to not want to believe that God's spiritual laws and instructions impact the physical realm in which we live to include our own physical health. One reason may be that we can't see the consequence/curse or reward/blessing immediately. Many people believe that because of Jesus' death and resurrection on the Cross, believers don't have to engage in spiritual warfare. We just accept God's sovereignty that He can do whatever He wants to, and we accept whatever comes our way until we get to heaven.

It is true that God is sovereign and can do whatever He wants to do; however, we limit God because we choose whether or not to pick up our responsibilities in response to His covenant with us.

Whether we believe or not, doesn't change the truth. For example, we can say, "I don't believe in germs because I can't see them," but when you are sick, you are eager to take an antibiotic to kill that germ. We teach our children to wash their hands at a very early age. Why? Because we believe that something invisible like a germ will eventually impact the visible natural realm, such as our body. We put a little gate up around our children or pets. Is it to restrict them to be spiteful or cause them to stumble, or is it to protect them from injury and death? Our view of God as Father will determine how we view His instructions.

Based on the whole counsel of God's Word, the entire Bible, and my personal relationship with Jesus, His Son, God our Father can be viewed through the following attributes:

- God is good!
- Everything God has for us and has done for us was accomplished through the sacrifice, shed blood, death and resurrection of His only Son, Jesus.
- God made each one of us significant. You are significant!

There is absolutely nothing impossible with God.

God's Covering Is Excellent

The commandments of God—the Words of God—are instructions to guide, mature, and protect His children (authentic, born-again, Spirit-filled followers of Jesus Christ) from being enticed and trapped by the enemy of God, Satan. Satan does not want you to fulfill your God-given purpose and destiny by sharing your testimonies with others so they would love God too. Satan does not want you to spend eternity with God but with him. He already knows that he will spend eternity in a dark fire pit with pain and agony, forever separated from God. His whole objective is to hurt God by enticing those God loves to be forever separated too.

For God so loved the world, that He gave His only begotten Son and whosoever believes in Him, will not perish, but have everlasting life (John 3:16).

God desires to be our God, our Healer, and our Deliverer. Because of Jesus' death, burial, and resurrection for our salvation, we can now choose between life or death, forever abiding with Jesus or forever cut off and separated from Him. But God loved us so much that He gave us direction, instruction, and healthy boundaries while on the earth for our success and protection. After the last person of Israel walked on dry ground through the Red Sea, Exodus 14 records that the waters that had been a wall to them, suddenly returned and covered up the Egyptians, killing all of them.

Thus the Lord saved Israel that day from the hand of the Egyptians, and Israel saw the Egyptians dead on the seashore. Israel saw the great power that the Lord used against the Egyptians, so the people feared the Lord, and they believed in the Lord and in his servant Moses (Exodus 14:30).

Authentic Christ followers have this same great power available to them because the spirit of the living God, Jesus, lives in them.

There the Lord made for them a statute and a rule, and there he tested them. saying, "if you will diligently listen to the voice of the Lord your God, and do that which is right in his eyes, and give ear to his commandments and keep all his statutes, I will put none of the diseases on you that I put on the Egyptians for I am the Lord, your healer" (Exodus 15:26-27).

It is recorded in history books that this was a period in history where there was no medicine used—the people relied only on the supernatural power of their God. They were completely cared for and lacked nothing. Of course, we know that everything hinged on not only faith but also obedience to God's instructions.

Trust and Obey

God Means What He Said

A few months after God delivered Moses and the people of Israel from Egypt, after He had established a relationship with them, God gave them foundational instructions that are true and relevant today. We know them as the Ten Commandments. Let's look at the first two commandments. These commandments set the foundation reflecting the dichotomy that I see today between the God of Abraham and Moses, as well as the New Testament disciples and the gods of our society for confessing Christ followers today.

> *And God spoke all these words, saying, "I am the Lord your God, who brought you out of the land of Egypt, out of the house of slavery. You shall have no other gods before me. You shall not make for yourself a carved image, or any likeness of anything that is in heaven above, or that is in the earth beneath, or that is in the water under the earth. You shall not bow down to them or serve them for the Lord your God am a jealous God, visiting the iniquity of the fathers on the children to the third and the fourth generation of those that hate me, but showing steadfast love to thousands of those who love me and keep my commandments"* (Exodus 20:1-5).

1. You shall have no other gods before me.

2. You shall not make for yourself an image or bow down or serve them, for I the Lord am a jealous God.

Idolatry (common definitions): anything that exalts itself above God; anything or anyone in which you place your trust, your desires and affections besides God; anything that replaces God in your priorities.

May I challenge you to a revelation that God has given me about trusting any other source of life except God (Genesis 1:7). As Christians, we commonly pray, "God, my life is in your hands." Is it really? Let the Lord help you discern what areas of your life are really in God's hands and which ones are in yours, or tragically in someone else's? God is drawing His people back to Him!

Let's look at why God is a jealous God when we look to other sources of life. We have been deceived that many things on this earth are God. They may be good things and some even beneficial, but they are not God!

As a nurse, I know first-hand what it means to practice health. Practice has never come close to being perfect. What is sad and dangerous is that medicine and pharmaceuticals were meant for the short-term treatment of symptoms—not for chronic, lifetime management. That is not healing. At its best, it is an attempt to add quality and length of days to a person. Rarely do you see a cure—and that is now called remission—no guarantee of the outcome because of so many variables. Again, healthcare professionals are the most compassionate and respected people I know, and the goal for all of us is to help people, alleviate suffering, and make someone whole again. There are so many drugs! The drugs have so many serious side effects that one really has to weigh the risks against the benefit. Many people do not really know the risks because they put so much trust in the drug and the person prescribing the drug or procedure.

I can no longer practice in giving people artificial or false hope, assuring them they should see improvement. Medical and mental health practices are causing people to be dependent on a counselor and/or drugs, hoping symptoms will be suppressed. No one is addressing the root cause of illness or cognitive behaviorial problems. Suicide is now considered an epidemic, yet totally preventable by giving the person hope.

No one seems to be able to figure it out. Why? Spiritual problems require spiritual solutions. What do people around us see? We share a gospel of hope and healing, but it appears to not be working. Why? Could it be when we do not believe the gospel we preach, that God doesn't notice? Could it be that the Jesus we are presenting is another Jesus, not the one that Paul described? The substance of faith hoped for and things not seen is a person—the substance, the assurance is Jesus! Apart from Christ, we have no hope! Drugs numb pain and kill people—Jesus desires to enter your situation and turn things around for His glory and to give LIFE. The world is watching!

The simplicity and message of the Gospel has not changed. Sickness, disease, anguish, and hopelessness came into the world originally through sin. God has dealt with sin—the root cause! Few really believe it! Healing, freedom and wellness are blessings from a relationship with a Father who loved us to forgive us our sins. That relationship and reconciliation to Him can only be found though loving and surrendering our lives to the Lordship of His Son, Jesus! Jesus paid the penalty so I could live! Faith is believing the One who gave us the promises.

For Christ did not send me to baptize but to preach the gospel, and not with words of eloquent wisdom lest the cross of Christ is emptied of its power. For the word of the Cross is folly to those perishing, but to us who are being saved, it is the power of God (1 Corinthians 1:17-18).

For I decided to know nothing except Jesus Christ and Him crucified... And my speech and my message were not in plausible words of wisdom, but in demonstration of the Spirit and power. So that your faith might not rest in the wisdom of men but in the power of God (1 Corinthians 2:2-5).

For the Kingdom of God does not consist in talk but in power (1 Corinthians 4:20).

For he himself is our peace (Ephesians 2:14).

As believers, we know the truth. We know that hope is a Person—Jesus—the perfect peace that only God can give. It is impossible for the world to give lasting hope and peace. Yet people are searching desperately, selling their souls for another worldview, product, or even another gospel!

Four

History of Medicine and Psychology

According to the *Handbook of Religion and Health Historical Timeline* (Koenig, King, and Carson 2012), the practice of medicine dates back to the pre-dynastic period in Egypt. Artifacts indicate that mental illness and physical illness were not distinguished from each other, both being understood in religious terms—demon possession. As Egyptian civilization developed in the Pharaonic times, there was little distinction between religion and magic and healing by laying on of hands to control factors in daily life. Hypnotism was used to influence the sick.

The first physician actually originated in ancient Egypt and his name was Imhotep. He lived during the Old Kingdom B.C., and he later was worshipped as a god. Massage therapy, physical medicine, and drug therapy were used to relieve pain. Deities were accepted as a way of life so that invoking their help was done first when treating medical conditions. Incantations were directly addressed to disease demons, commanding them to leave the body.

Hinduism then emerged out of India and similarly to the Chinese religions, life was controlled by the spiritual world, and both countries used incantations, amulets, drugs, rituals, herbs, even cow by products to cure illness. And all these were performed by a priest. Acupuncture was a method used in China, where they tapped into what they still believe as the body's energy (life force) channels and anatomical connections to bring healing.

All this was going on when Abraham was called by God, and

the monotheist religious tradition of Judaism emerged (and later, Islam and Christianity).

Out of Bondage and Into God's Provision—No Plan B!

In Psalm 107 we see that God had a redemptive plan from the beginning. Because of their iniquities (unbelief), His children suffered affliction; but each time they cried out in their trouble, God delivered them from their distress. Verse 43 ends with "Whoever is wise let him attend to these things; let them consider the steadfast love of the Lord."

According to the *Handbook of Religion and Health*, in the Old Testament times the sick were examined and kept under careful observation by the priest. Biblical medicine is exclusively supernaturalistic; no other naturalistic medicine paradigm developed as seen in other ancient cultures.

In another secular history book entitled, *Nursing the Finest Art: An Illustrated History*, M. Patricia Donahue describes the Hebrew culture as people who embraced a theocentric philosophy, a belief in a personal God and monotheistic. Their strength was derived from belief in the one true God. These philosophies taught that humans have a free will and an immortal soul created by God, and that a human being is a body, mind, and spirit unity. The Hebrew people abhorred the innumerable deities of other nations. They denounced superstitions and magical practices to the extent that death was the penalty for performing them. State and church were under the same head—a theocratic government (officials who are regarded as divinely guided).

Donahue goes on to describe that all power over life and death was in the hands of Jehovah. God became the source of health, and its preservation was to be found in "keeping before the Lord." A way of living emerged that did not necessitate specific medical practices. Can you see? God really did take care of His people!

Later, Hippocrates is introduced as the Father of Medicine; he was Greek and practiced traditions foreign to God. Alchemists produced mixtures or drugs from elements of earth—chemicals and minerals—to treat illness, even though mental health was thought to be demonic. The word *pharmakia* is a Greek word meaning sorcery, witchcraft, poison, and drugs. The Bible calls out sorcery and witchcraft as opposing God.

Psychology (the study of the psyche—soul) has a very dark origin. It actually started out as a subgroup under philosophy and is fairly recent compared to medicine. Many of the early psychologists were not believers in God; or if they did, they made it clear that psychology and religion should be separate. Many psychologists promoted opinions that religion caused mental illness. Some believed that the only way to treat someone with religious values is to treat their mental illness like you would with someone that has a chronic disease.

One of the most stunning findings for me over the years is the fact that individuals such as Carl Jung, for example, influenced teaching and philosophies that have become a foundation for many modern tools used today and even in our churches. Carl Jung is known to be the Father of Psychoanalysis. One can go to his foundation's website today and read the vast array of his publications. The sad fact is that in his own stories and writings, he described his years of mystical experiences of entering into the spirit realm and talking to people such as Elijah, Salome, and his spirit guide named Philemon. He describes how he received all his inspiration from his spirit guide, whom he described as being as real as you and I sitting across from each other talking. These encounters gave him inspirational knowledge to describe human types or personalities, thus later, the foundation of the Meyers-Briggs Personality Assessment, as well as his theory of unconsciousness.

The following is a sample from the resource page of the Carl

Jung Foundation: www.CarlJung.net for his theory of unconsciousness.

> Though initially Jung followed the Freudian theory of unconscious as the psychic strata formed by repressed wishes, he later developed his own theory on the unconscious to include some new concepts. The most important of them is the archetype.
>
> Archetypes constitute the structure of the collective unconscious - they are psychic innate dispositions to experience and represent basic human behavior and situations. The most important of all is the Self, which is the archetype of the Center of the psychic person, his/her totality or wholeness.
>
> The collective unconscious is a universal datum, that is, every human being is endowed with this psychic archetype-layer since his/her birth. One cannot acquire this strata by education or other conscious effort because it is innate. We may also describe it as a universal library of human knowledge, or the sage in man, the very transcendental wisdom that guides mankind. Religious experience must be linked with the experience of the archetypes of the collective unconscious. Thus, God himself is lived like a psychic experience of the path that leads one to the realization of his/her psychic wholeness.

Much controversy exists in psychology still today, not only from the medical community but also those that embrace Christianity. There are arguments as to whether or not there is real empirical or scientific data. Labeling is based on groups of psychologists and psychiatrists categorizing observations and putting names to them so that they can substantiate or validate a 'secular' medical existence, diagnosis, and treatment for a behavior they really don't understand. There is little or no empirical scientific evidence of any of these labels, only observation. Once a label has been made and a subsequent code identified for that label, the professional can prescribe treatment to include a drug, and bill accordingly.

What is startling, is that this small group of professionals now dictates to the public what is considered mental illness or not; what is considered normal or not. This team of professionals now have become experts for deciding court cases, making foster parenting rules for a family, and deeming a person incompetent or mentally ill.

Psychiatry and psychology prescribe medications that are very dangerous and tell us that the cause of the labeled mental disease is a chemical imbalance. But what is the source of the chemical imbalance? It has been widely known for many years that any type of stress will cause physiological changes, for example, blood glucose to increase, that is not new. Symptoms are managed, but the source of the stress still remains problematic. Could it be that spiritual problems require spiritual solutions?

Mental health professionals have admitted to me personally as well as publically that drugs increase the risk and contribute greatly to the suicide epidemic that is currently plaguing America. The mental health system is not working.

As a nurse and a minister, I see first-hand these treatments generally not working. People are experiencing depression, suicidal ideation, paranoia, aggression, violent thoughts, hallucinations, mood and personality changes, insomnia, agitation, and impulsivity—the very side effects that are listed as possibilities. People actually tell you their body is not right. Many people do not want to take medication, but they are told that the medicine is their only hope. The drugs can stay in the body systems for months after discontinuation. Parents also express that they do not want their children on medications, but feel forced to do so through fear and intimidation. Parents are told that their kids cannot enter school and are fearful of having their children taken away from them if they refuse behavioral or cognitive drugs as well as vaccinations, using the term harm and neglect. Wow!

The Citizen's Commission on Human Rights

The Citizen's Commission on Human Rights (CCHR) was originally formed in 1969 as a global watchdog committed to investigating and exposing human rights violations in the field of mental health. They have been instrumental in legislative and practice reforms that help protect people. Their reported examples of these reforms are the restriction and monitoring of the use of patient restraints to include chemical restraint; informed consent for treatment and the right to legal representation and advocacy; prohibition of forcing parents to put children on psychiatric drugs to address behavioral issues; and strong warnings for drugs like antidepressants that can cause suicidal thoughts and actions in persons with no previous history of psychosis.

The CCHR (http://www.cchr.org) has many resources and reports of the avoidable drug-related deaths and what is termed abuse from psychiatry. They promote themselves as activists for parents and children and those that don't have a voice in their victimization of being labeled, drugged, or receiving electroshock therapy.

This organization calls psychiatry a death industry because of the common side effects of psychiatric drugs to include mania, psychosis, hallucinations, depersonalization, suicidal ideation, heart attack, stroke, and sudden death. It is shocking to know this is happening and we allow it. It is a testimony that our society no longer values human life the same way as God, our heavenly Father, does.

This highly informative website lists resources for public education and for people to be able to identify the dangers and side effects of each drug that they attribute as destroying people rather than helping them. One such resource on the website listed the prescription drugs the gunmen were taking at the time of each incident such as the Columbine School and Virginia Tech School tragedies. CCHR reported that data from more recent tragedies are no longer available to this agency to post on their website for public review. CCHR suggests these young people were taking dangerous drugs that cause things like hallucinations, paranoia, delusion, impulsivity, aggression, and violence. Coincidence? You decide.

At the website, CCHR describes various ways psychiatry and subsequent drugs are causing death and destruction: death of a child due to long-term usage of a stimulant drug used for attention disorder; a loss of a loved one by a gun used by a teenager prescribed a violence-inducing psychiatric drug; an elderly person's death from electroshock therapy or a prescribed antipsychotic drug prescribed in a nursing home. This organization makes bold statements and is a wealth of information regarding mental health practices and abuse, as well as legislative activity relating to parent and patient rights around the world. Despite these serious problems, the system for mental health diagnoses and treatments is widely accepted as the benchmark for both judging and treating human behavior.

The Citizens Commission on Human Rights lists the following as facts: http://www.cchr.org/quick-facts/no-genetic-proof-of-mental-illnesses.html

- Psychiatric disorders are not medical diseases.
- Psychiatry has never established the cause of any mental disorder.
- The theory that mental disorders derive from chemical imbalances in the brain is unproven opinion, not fact.
- The brain is the not the real cause of life's problems.

In addition, these are example posts on this webpage as they substantiate facts that one should know about psychiatry:

> It is well established that the drugs used to treat a mental disorder, for example, may induce long-lasting biochemical and even structural changes [including in the brain], which in the past were claimed to be the cause of the disorder, but may actu-

ally be an effect of the treatment. —*Dr. Elliot Valenstein, Biopsychologist, Author, Blaming the Brain*

Psychiatry's claim that mental illnesses are brain diseases is a claim supposedly based on recent discoveries in neuroscience, made possible by [brain] imaging techniques for diagnosis and pharmacological agents for treatment. This is not true. —*Dr. Thomas Szasz, Professor Emeritus of Psychiatry, New York University Medical School, Syracuse*

There are increasing concerns among the clinical community that…neuroscientific developments [do] not reveal anything about the nature of psychiatric disorders…. —*Dr. David Healy, Psychiatrist, Director of the North Wales Department of Psychological Medicine*

…modern psychiatry has yet to convincingly prove the genetic/biologic cause of any single mental illness…Patients [have] been diagnosed with "chemical imbalances" despite the fact that no test exists to support such a claim, and…there is no real conception of what a correct chemical balance would look like. —*Dr. David Kaiser, Psychiatrist*

There's no biological imbalance. When people come to me and they say, "I have a biochemical imbalance," I say, "Show me your lab tests." There are no lab tests. So what's the biochemical imbalance? —*Dr. Ron Leifer, Psychiatrist*

Psychiatry makes unproven claims that depression, bipolar illness, anxiety, alcoholism and a host of other disorders are in fact primarily biologic and probably genetic in origin…This kind of faith in science and progress is staggering, not to mention naïve and perhaps delusional. —*Dr. David Kaiser, Psychiatrist*

The theories are held on to not only because there is nothing else to take their place, but also because they are useful in promoting drug treatment. —*Dr. Elliott Valenstein Ph.D., Author, Blaming the Brain*

I believe, until the public and psychiatry itself see that DSM labels are not only useless as medical "diagnoses" but also have the potential to do great harm—particularly when they are used as means to deny individual freedoms, or as weapons by psychiatrists acting as hired guns for the legal system. —*Dr. Sydney Walker III, Psychiatrist*

No biochemical, neurological, or genetic markers have been found for Attention Deficit Disorder, Oppositional Defiant Disorder, Depression, Schizophrenia, anxiety, compulsive alcohol and drug abuse, overeating, gambling or any other so-called mental illness, disease, or disorder. —*Bruce Levine, Ph.D., Psychologist, Author, Commonsense Rebellion*

Unlike medical diagnoses that convey a probable cause, appropriate treatment and likely prognosis, the disorders listed in DSM-IV are terms arrived at through peer consensus. —*Tana Dineen Ph.D., Canadian Psychologist*

The danger with all disciplines is that research is based on a hypothesis (theory, an assumption if you will) that must be proved. Few things are actually proven because there are too many variables that cannot be defined nor controlled. Many studies are not actually statistically significant. What happens, though, is people promote insufficient conclusions or data, not producing significance, as general truth to the public. People put their trust in practitioners prescribing drugs and treatments that they trust are going to work or cure them, and the practitioners know the success and failures of each. The best practitioners can do is temporarily attempt to manage a person's illness. Little is done to remove the root cause or prevent the problem from reoccurring or ever occurring in the first place.

In many professions, especially mental health, treatments and interventions are centered around changing one's environment, behavior, capabilities, and even an attempt to change belief systems—all do not work—these things leave even Christians frustrated and stuck. God instructs us that until we understand and know that our identity is in Him, as sons and daughters, then any human effort or attempt to replace Him will never satisfy or set people free. When one knows their identity in Christ—there is no room for depression, anxiety, gender confusion, or any other type of confusion! But of course, God also tells us that many will not believe or follow Him and will mock and call us foolish.

But the world is watching! One can't blame compassionate care professionals for trying. In modern times, we too have a problem proving our Gospel. It really comes down to where the rubber meets the road. Do we believe the Gospel we preach? Do we prove that the Gospel is true? Can people believe that Jesus is alive by our testimonies? Psalms 107 says that when the people cried out to God in their troubles, He was faithful to deliver them from their distress because of His steadfast love for them.

Post-Truth Society

We are living not only in a post-Christian world but also a post-Truth society. Truth is only truth if it serves one well, otherwise one will reject it as truth. In other words, whatever you perceive is truth, or want to believe is truth, is truth.

Practicing medicine and psychology are unending, exhausting, highly costly, and frankly, dangerous! The foundational truths that govern humanistic and spirituality philosophies are founded on ancient methodologies and mythology, universalism, and knowledge from man. Giving oneself over to another person to allow the mind or body to be placed in altered states of consciousness or manipulated; or to place the body to be subject to practice by theories and drugs (toxins) promising cures are not ways founded on Truth. In a society that already testifies that it has no value for human life, how do we follow these practices?

There are over 300 theoretical approaches/methods in which therapists or counselors can use. Most choose one or two that best work for them. One may never know what is being used when you choose a therapist unless the individual therapist promotes the behavioral conceptual framework in which he/she practices.

But God cares about the truth of our well-being—He is Truth! God created, redeemed, restored, and sustains us. No assumptions or theories here—we are His workmanship! God wants us well! He fearfully and wonderfully designed us to be well and fruitful.

> *But God, being rich in mercy, because of the great love with which he loved us, even when we were dead in our trespasses, made us alive together with Christ—by grace you have been saved—and raised us up with him and seated us with him in the heavenly places in Christ Jesus, so that in the coming ages he might show the immeasurable riches of his grace in kindness toward us in Christ Jesus. For by grace you have been saved through faith. And this is not your own doing; it is the gift of God, not a result of works, so that no one may boast.* **For we are his workmanship, created in Christ Jesus for good works, which God prepared beforehand, that we should walk in them** (Ephesians 2:4-10).

Nothing New Under the Sun

All through history, natural theories began to replace or blend the religious explanations of Egypt, Greece, and other foreign traditions, as men reduced the immortal soul to consciousness and thought. Some philosophers built theories such that the whole universe can be explained in terms of physical laws or within the realm of unconsciousness, all the while claiming the discoveries came from the Holy Spirit and other spirit guides. Thus the church holds the position that secular methods of cure are God-given and work through the exercise of God's power.

Finally, in the Age Enlightenment, 1700-1800, traditional religious values and beliefs are challenged further. Reason is viewed as the essence of human nature, and science a way to explain the universe. There is no further need of God.

It was a sad day when ministers and priests began handing the souls of men over to psychiatry and medicine, trusting various professions intentionally without God to make one well.

The Hebrew children and the first century disciples would despise such rituals and practices, and they certainly didn't need them. They belonged to God—the God who created them. They knew their God. They did not have situational faith to believe but developed relational trust on their God who provided, healed, delivered, redeemed, and empowered them to live whole with innermost peace that only He can provide. They faced obstacles that we in America can't even fathom, yet they overcame and the rest of the world knew it. We now read it in secular history books, as well as the Holy Bible.

References

Ravenhill, D: *For God's Sake Listen: A Prophetic Word to the Church*, 2013, Offspring Publishers.

Bonnke, R: *Holy Spirit: Are We Flammable or Fireproof?* Orlando, 2017, Christ For All Nations.

Koenig, H., King, C. and Carson, V: *The Handbook of Religion and Health*, 2012, Oxford University Press.

Donahue, MP: *Nursing the Finest Art: An Illustrated History*, St. Louis, 1996, The CV Mosby Company.

Citizen's Commission on Human Rights (CCHR) website: http://www.cchr.org

Carl Jung Foundation Website: www.CarlJung.net

Five

Spiritual Psychology: Your Invitation to the Occult

Transpersonal Psychology, aka Self Transformation, aka Spiritual Psychology, aka Psycho-Occult, aka Metaphysics, aka New Age, aka Contemplative Meditation, aka Mindfulness

The fusion of psychology and spirituality has become one of today's most popular systems and therapy for self-understanding and self-actualization. Many false doctrines, philosophies, and practices are infiltrating the church, causing confusion and apostasy leading people to spiritual death.

One such spiritual psychology approach to life is the ancient symbol of the Sacred Enneagram. It is being introduced as a powerful new way to use the Enneagram as a tool for personal transformation and spiritual growth. It is being promoted and packaged to the Christian community as a personality typing system that shows how to overcome inner barriers to inner freedom. In addition, one can realize unique gifts that match one's own unique spiritual path to God. What is more alarming is that it is quickly being embraced with biblical concepts redefined and false contextual interpretations of Scripture. Believers are trusting their pastors, mentors, coaches, and leaders to guide them in truth. What is happening, though, is apostasy—misled believers are choosing a different spiritual path than what the Bible teaches through Jesus Christ.

One of many books teaching about the wisdom and power of

Spiritual Psychology: Your Invitation to the Occult

the sacred Enneagram, is the book, *The Sacred Enneagram: Finding Your Unique Path to Spiritual Growth* by Christopher L. Heuertz. It is being used for church leadership development and as a tool for discipleship in spiritual growth for those in their sphere of influence. The Enneagram Tradition is a type of course one would now find in some divinity programs. The Enneagram is a geometrical symbol that has symbols within it and is a complex system of understanding individuals. It is described as a powerful, dynamic, and open system of various typologies and offers itself as a path to liberation or self-actualization through unique spiritual pathways to God based on the individual's personality type. It is being promoted by Enneagram teachers as a profoundly new fusion of psychology and spirituality that offers an exciting vision of human possibility and a clear map of the different spiritual paths so that a person can reach their highest self-expression.

This book and the sacred Enneagram are clearly far more than a personality test or self-reflection. It is promoted as a way in which Christians can grow closer to God. It is considered sacred because one's enneagram type isn't fundamentally about the type of person we are, but it is a pathway back to God—a path back to one's true self. Through this system or spiritual journey, one is taught prayer postures and ways to pray that are unique to the type or path one is seeking. When they find their true self, they also find themselves in communion with God.

The sacred Enneagram system renders false interpretation and integration of God's Word to purposely begin the deception of Christian thought and practice. For example with the Beatitudes, the nine fruit of the Spirit, and nine gifts of the Spirit, the author or spiritual leader makes analogies with terms such as Virtues and Holy Ideas. The false rendering is that the Bible is affirming evidence of one's wholeness through peace of mind and one's heart as revealed through Virtues and Holy Ideas to become who we were created to be.

A Greek contemporary of the Buddha, philosopher and mathematician Pythagoras, who studied in Egypt, fused mysticism and mathematics and developed the Law of Three. He used the Enneagram symbol for his spiritual signature after learning it had meaning from the worship of the Ennead (nine deities of ancient Egyptian mythology (Heuertz, C. 2017).

Danger! Satan So Badly Wants To Be God

There is obvious spiritual danger with the philosophy and source of spiritual wisdom being embraced through this tool. The Enneagram tool and ideas go back to ancient eastern mysticism and are used in other Eastern traditional beliefs and in multiple religions such as Buddhism and Hinduism. And again, according to history, the Enneagram was used in ancient Babylon and Egypt! Throughout the Bible we see God's abomination against God's people mixing with other religions and philosophies of thought—the mixing of what God calls holy and what is the profane. God is not pleased and will one day vindicate His name.

One of the core lies in this philosophy is one's identity. In this belief system, one is taught that our sense of identity and who we think we are is only an illusion—*a false self*. One must be awakened to the *true self*. The Enneagram is taught to offer a sacred map for our souls—a map that when understood, leads us home to our true identity and to God. The Enneagram is described as the aid to wake one up. The author further indicated that the Sacred Enneagram offers nine mirrors for self-reflection, and if one chooses to gaze into it directly, it will shake loose the illusions that caused one to be lost. It teaches that truth is hard to find when it has been hidden so long behind one's personality. A person's personality is hidden behind a mask—taking off the mask begins the spiritual journey. Through this process and tool, one is expected to find direction for one's inner restlessness and find peace and rest in just being.

Spiritual Psychology: Your Invitation to the Occult

Another of many more core lies is the source of the wisdom. Many times in these philosophies you see the terms "masters of wisdom" or "seekers of truth" in the quest for enlightenment or awakening into full consciousness. Spiritual leaders throughout history used the enneagram for divination, receiving personal spirit revelations of demonic power and a tool for personal transformation in both conscious and unconscious states. One does not even know the damage one is doing to a person's soul (will, mind, emotions) when ministers refer people to counselors or organizations for spiritual or mental assistance. When people embrace these philosophies and engage in their mindfulness activities, they are being drawn away from God.

Through the prophet Isaiah, God clearly states that wisdom, understanding, and counsel are from the Holy Spirit (Isaiah 11:2 NKJV). Jude 25 (NKJV) says,

To God our Savior, who alone is wise, be glory, and majesty, dominion and power, both now and forever. Amen.

I hope you can see that Satan is the counterfeit God and Holy Spirit in this system of thought and the spiritual exercises and experiences. It is no different from when he was in the Garden with Adam and Eve. He lured them into thinking they were missing out on something and could be like God. Satan captivated Eve's heart to look to something else than what God instructed. This time it is no different, except he is luring people to look within themselves to find and become who they were made to be—like God. Satan knows he is coming to the home stretch with his existence in this world; and through this deception, he can become the master of one's soul.

It is like a Ouija board—one is asking questions and someone else is guiding, which we already know is demonic. The same anti-Christ spirit is guiding innocent, misled, sincere searching people who think they are seeking and serving God. The system tells them that everything they have constructed in their minds, emotions, and beliefs must be deconstructed because it is a false self. The reconstruction is done through this tool and the false philosophies taught, resulting in spiritual experiences that bring them to a new reality of self. The new beliefs render people vulnerable, and they see themselves as not needing a Savior because God's name is Love. The God they think they are finding is really Satan.

As a watchman, I pray and grieve with God. I am so grieved over the believers that are embracing this occult spirituality and tool for their lives. This philosophy plays into the behaviors, emotions, and feelings of people. Sadly, it actually describes the condition of the human race after the spiritual death of Adam and Eve which caused all mankind to be separated from God. It describes not just the personalities of people but depicts people who are empty and lost and in need of a Savior. Using this psycho-spiritual attraction, Satan has come up with his own counterfeit redemptive plan—he is the savior so there is no need for Jesus.

Jesus' shedding His blood on the cross to restore all that was lost and drawing men back to communion with God is a myth in Satan's plan. Do you see the parallel of the counterfeit? In this Enneagram spiritual journey, one is expecting to find their unique path to commune with God. The Enneagram system uses invitation, consent (person must agree), and engage (person actively participates) as terms we would use for salvation and discipleship. Traditional Christianity is rejected as the same redundant stories in the Bible that become old and boring. Thus, such a belief system simply won't last, and one will be restless and searching.

An invitation to engage the Enneagram is blatantly found on the inside cover of the book, *The Sacred Enneagram* (Heuertz. C. 2017). It describes the Enneagram as being there to help one find their identity, better relate to others, and find God. The author calls this symbol a pathway to the souls and promotes that it reveals nine ways to find your true self and to God. It further promotes this sacred symbol as something that will help you understand yourself, move you toward spiritual growth, and awaken your unique gifts. It ends with the sacred Enneagram as your invitation to begin a journey of life transformation!

My heart is grieved and I pray with groaning over those that embrace the Enneagram and its many pathways to God. In deception, they will find at the end of the pathway another master than Jesus. The stakes are high! At the end this journey, people will find themselves in bondage and forever still spiritually lost and separated from the Father who so loved them, the Father who gave His only Son, Jesus, to die so that each could choose Him and not perish. In John 14:6, Jesus clearly states that He is the only Way, the truth, and the life and that no man can come to the Father, but by Him (Jesus)!

There Is Hope! We Carry Hope!

A born-again, spirit-filled disciple of Jesus Christ carries hope. We pray! We know that God intervenes on our behalf. When God sent His Son to carry the sins of the world, God gave us Him. Jesus, the Hope of the world, resides in us. It is critical for God's children to grow up and walk in the fullness of His deity as the first century disciples did.

We have created a culture of *self* as God and a culture of accommodation. People are more interested in themselves than others or even God. People tell us what they want to see in churches so that we can attract them. And we strive constantly to keep them. In reality, people are innately searching for God. Innate attributes that Adam had before his sin alienated him, now have become man's deep needs and only God can fill those needs. Jesus came to restore all that Adam lost. For example, after Adam's sin alienated him from God:

- *Acceptance* was replaced by rejection; therefore we all have a need to belong.

- *Innocence* was replaced by guilt and shame; therefore the need for a legitimate sense of worth had to be restored for us.
- *Dominion* was replaced by weakness and helplessness. therefore we all have a need for strength and self-control.

God has fully restored those to Himself who choose to surrender their life to Jesus.

Colossians 1:1-12, 19 says that we can be filled with the knowledge of God's will in all wisdom and spiritual understanding that we may walk worthy of the Lord and pleasing to Him, being fruitful in every good work and increasing in the knowledge of God. It tells us that we are strengthened with all might according to His glorious power for all patience and longsuffering. It goes on to say that God qualified us to be partakers of our heavenly inheritance! He delivered or rescued us from the tyranny and power of the kingdom of darkness and placed us in His Kingdom, the kingdom of His Son, Jesus. It is through Jesus whom we have redemption through His blood for the forgiveness of sins. And verse 19 reminds us that it pleased the Father!

Warning! Warning! Don't Be Deceived!

Colossians 2 warns us not to let anyone deceive us with words but for us to be steadfast in our faith. He warns not to let anyone cheat us through philosophy or empty deceit, according to the tradition of men and the principles of this world. We do not find God through the philosophies of man nor through meditation as we look inward to reflect and become aware of ourselves. It is through Jesus Christ and Him alone that we can find God and start a new life. He makes it very clear in Colossians 2:8-10 (NKJV) that it is not philosophy but Jesus Christ and *He only* is the basis of our faith. For in Jesus Christ dwells all the fullness of the Godhead (Father, Son, and Holy Spirit). The great news is that Colossians 10 concludes with "and you are complete in Him who is the head of all principality and power." That means our identity comes from Jesus and is complete in Jesus! That is awesome! Wow!

In fact 1 John 4:17 (NKJV) says that possessing this perfected love in Jesus results in fearless confidence toward God, that we don't have to fear the coming day of judgment like the rest of the world will. God even says that *as He is, so are we in this world!*

The devil knows what we have and to whom we belong. He is evil and crafty and hates you! He will try to do anything He can to distract you from being a fully devoted follower of Christ. He will diligently and subtly turn your heart to embrace a Christianized occult practice or philosophy. The spiritual path will deconstruct what you know to be true and reconstruct a new reality for you that leads one to blindly renounce Jesus and become enslaved to the world of Satan.

If You Hear Any Other Gospel, It Is Cursed!

Our identity in Christ is the starting point of the beginning of a new life for our spiritual journey. Spiritual psychology of the Enneagram teaches a total opposite. This psycho-spirituality teaches that we live a false self view or an illusion if we believe our identity is in Christ. We know the truth is that in Christ we have been restored and walk in communion with Abba Father, Jesus, and the Holy Spirit. We are not still lost. Spiritual psychology, such as the sacred Enneagram tradition, persuades one to believe that we are lost and have to be found. They use the analogy of Dorothy in the Wizard of Oz living in a false reality, searching to go home. When you become awakened, you will be in your true self reality. This is dangerous teaching because it is a blatant perversion of the Gospel, and the Bible calls it cursed!

New Testament disciples such as Paul, John, and Jude warned us of a false gospel coming into the church. Psychology and spirituality create a perversion of the true Gospel of Jesus Christ that Paul warned us about in 1 Corinthians 11:4. He said if you hear any other gospel, it is accursed! In other words it doesn't matter how sincere or how credentialed a person might be, or how charismatic something seems, or if it contains a lot of truth. *If the message is not the death of sin through the cross of Jesus Christ, let it be cursed!* The word "spirituality" does not mean Jesus, God, or the Holy Spirit of the Bible. Many assume that if something is spiritual and is taught in connection with the Bible, it is the true gospel being represented.

Jude appeared urgent in his purpose to warn a community of Christians against false teachers, some even in the church. As in the other Gospels, Jude describes these leaders as sensual (means interested in self, not having the Holy Spirit); they were perverting the truth, deceiving people, and they were destined for divine judgment. Lastly, they were making promises on which they could not deliver. Jude tells us to contend earnestly (keep close guard) for the faith which was once and for all delivered to the saints. In other words, guard what God has taught and given you! False teachers within a community seek to overthrow the faith of God's people. Many teachers may be walking in deception themselves and replicating deception.

In Jude 5 we are reminded, even though we already once knew it, the Lord saved the people out of the land of Egypt, and afterward destroyed those who did not believe. In Jude 16-20 God tells us again to remember the words that were spoken through the apostles of our Lord Jesus Christ because He knew of the forthcoming apostasy and mocking of our faith in our Lord Jesus Christ.

The word "Lord" (Strong's #1203 *despotes*) signifies owner, master, one who has absolute dominion, supreme authority, and unlimited power arising from ownership. Despotes includes total submission on our part to God's will, not out of slavish fear or bondage, but willingly with joy. Do you see why it is imperative that we don't submit ourselves to any other authority, spirit, or teaching?

Guard Your Soul (Mind, Will, and Emotions)

Jude wraps his writing up with more good news for those of us that surrender our life under the Lordship of Jesus Christ. God says that His power is able to keep us from falling; however, our responsibility is to build ourselves up in the truth through praying in the Holy Spirit to anticipate our final salvation (forever with Him). God already resides in you. You are His temple on this earth. Pray, led by the Holy Spirit. Pray in tongues—your heavenly language—often, not just daily. Romans 8:38-39 (NKJV) reminds us that nothing—no angel nor principality can separate us from God's love that is found in His Son Jesus!

I beseech you therefore brethren by the mercies of God that you present your bodies a living sacrifice, holy and acceptable to God, which is your reasonable service. 2) And do not be conformed to this world, but transformed by the renewing or your mind, that you may prove what is that good and acceptable and perfect will of God (Romans 12:1-2 NKJV).

The word "conformed" (Strong's #4964 *suschematizo*) means to accommodate oneself to a model or pattern. This word appears only one other time in the New Testament in 1 Peter 1:14 within the context of worldly lusts. Any apparent or superficial conformity to the present world system or any accommodation to its ways would be fatal to the Christian life *(Kingdom Dynamics, New Spirit Filled Bible,* NKJV*).*

Do you see why the enemy wants so badly for you to deny or reject Jesus as Lord? Of course, you wouldn't think of doing that! However, the deception is that through these philosophies, you are led to believe you are still loving and serving God. It wouldn't be called deception if you were not blinded to the absolute truth. The deception is that you have now consented to the invitation to participate in the kingdom of darkness. The Holy Spirit will be replaced by spirit guides, in other words, demons. The voices and experiences will not always be God.

The Bible is replete with prophecy describing the end-times. There will be liars who come in and sear men's consciousness through their lies. *Protect your mind!* Take inventory to what and whom you are inviting into your life. Also, take inventory to know what and to whom you are giving consent by participation in offerings of spiritual growth or wellness initiatives, heart/mind/body teachings, activities, or exercises. Deception would not be deception if there were not truth involved. If one doesn't have a foundation in scriptural truth, one doesn't know to separate when truth is compromised.

Blending and mixing belief systems and philosophies and the ways of the world with what God says is the most dangerous deception of all. We become desensitized to evil, and it becomes difficult to discern truth. The standard and authority will always be the Bible—what does God say?

A mixture spiritually is just as good as pure evil. If you had a glass of water and put dirt in it, would you drink it? God won't. Jesus said in 1 John 1:5 that there is no darkness in Him. You must carve out spiritual boundaries for yourself and recognize that there are spiritual absolutes for your life so that you are not setting yourself and your families up to be prey!

Being ignorant of the spirituality deity and doctrine behind a teaching or exercise, or believing that your intent is not spiritual and really doesn't matter, are not excuses. Your intent is irrelevant, and you consent by mere participation, which invites the demonic realm into your life. It will negatively affect you.

Renew Your Mind in the Knowledge of God by the Word of God

To renew the mind is to restore it to freshness and its original state, implying God's redemptive power to reinstate features of God's original intent for humanity and a recovery of man's potentialities before the fall. We renew our minds in the knowledge of

God by reading and hearing His Word, which is spirit and life (John 6:63). The Holy Spirit is He who ushers the Kingdom of God into our lives. He will guide you, teach you, and tell you of things to come through God's Word and revelation that is always consistent with His Word. He is our Teacher, Counselor, Comforter, the giver of spiritual gifts, and He fills us with His power.

Declare with me: I am equipped with the full armor of God (Ephesians 6:13), packed full of the Holy Spirit, with more than enough power inside of me to raise the dead (Romans 8:11), heal the sick, and cast out devils (Matthew 10:1). My faith can move mountains (Mark 11:23), my words contain life and death (Proverbs 18:21), and my life was bought at a price—Jesus covered it (1 Corinthians 6:20)! Thank You, Jesus!

Guard What God Has Given You

Guard earnestly what God has given you! Jude v. 24 and 25 end with giving glory to God.

> Now to Him who is able to keep you from stumbling, and to present you faultless before the presence of His glory with exceeding joy. To God our Savior, who alone is wise, be glory and majesty, dominion and power, both now and forever. Amen.

The word "able" (*dunamai* Strong's #1410) means to have power. Then combine power with willingness, inherent strength, and action. Power, strength, and action! Who would want to be anywhere else but in God's Kingdom? He takes great care over His sons and daughters, and He watches over His Word to perform it (Jeremiah 1:12). Contend for your faith—guard earnestly and diligently what God has given you!

Where Are You?

This is the same question God asked Adam and He is asking you today. He knew where Adam and Eve were hiding in the garden—He's God! The question He was asking is do you know now where you are in relationship to God? That is always the question regarding your position in relationship to Christ and is the critical, defining line that determines who belongs to Him for all eternity. Matthew 7:13-14 (NKJV) says that the road that leads to life is narrow and difficult, and few will find it. I believe it is because of the mixture, blending, and syncretism causing lack of discernment that many will be found saying, "But Lord, I did all these things in Your name." And He will respond, "Depart from Me, I never knew you." In other words, "You chose not to make Me your Lord!" For you see He warns us that broad is the way that leads to destruction and many will take it. He is very serious that He is Lord! God will never share His essence or glory with another outside of His Son, Jesus Christ. Spiritual mixing of any kind is not acceptable. We are to not have any fellowship with evil.

If you have realized you have been dabbling or participating or leading in a spiritual psychology teaching, prayer posture, activity, or exercise using the wisdom or a tool, such as the sacred Enneagram, or any type of worldview occultism, metaphysical or complementary "Christian" philosophy, it is not too late to repent and run away from it. Now! Please! Run away from it!

We are at the door of the last day judgment. Do not confuse God's patience with indifference. Be careful to heed God's perspective on situations in which you find yourself. Set your heart to see God's external perspective for evil will be punished. Malachi 2:18 says that at that Judgment, the righteous and the wicked will be clearly distinguishable as those who serve God and those who do not. Those that fear the Lord—fear His name—there will be protection and healing in His wings. Choose this day to honor, worship, and serve Jesus and have no foreign alliances with other gods.

If you are presently under leadership that participates in or promotes personal or spiritual inventory tools and philosophies for coaching or spiritual growth, get yourself out from under it quickly.

Spiritual Psychology: Your Invitation to the Occult

The stakes are too high. Satan, the master deceiver, is studying you and capturing your soul, and you don't realize it. Imagine yourself outside reaching down to pick some beautiful flowers, and suddenly you noticed a snake gazing into your eyes ready to pounce his fangs on your neck. What would you do? You would drop everything in your hands, back up, turn around and run, even if it meant accidentally bruising a couple of people you knocked over in your haste to get away. This is the scenario when you have opened a spiritual door by inviting satanic forces into your life, space, or home. You must choose to renounce the practice and shut the door and run to Jesus!

You must choose the fear of the Lord over the fear of man! Many of you have taken a child to get a vaccine. The child throws a fit—cries, bites, kicks, or even may have to be held down to get the injection because it hurts! Do we just say, "Oh well, maybe another time" or "Oh well, their children's pastor will take care of it eventually?" How silly. You would be aggressive in your actions to get the vaccine. Spiritually, we can no longer be passive about each other or with our walk with God. Yes, it hurts sometimes to hear truth. Yes, it hurts to lose friends that think you are not practical. Yes, it hurts risking to lose relationships with people close to you who may perceive you are questioning their faith or preaching to them. It is okay. Our focus must be eternity. Those that are walking in truth will know you care for them.

The Holy Bible is the only source of truth. It is the only spiritual road map to God. It is the only mirror you need to see yourself. God's Word is the only way to obtain your personal or spiritual gifting inventory. God's Word is the only word you need for marriage counseling, raising your children, and is the best medicine. God's Word is the absolute authority for your soul and a successful life, now and into eternity.

The book of Jude (v. 1-25) sums it up perfectly. Jude was speaking specifically to "those who are called sanctified by God the

Father, and preserved in Jesus Christ..." (v. 2). Today, perpetrators of unbiblical standards and false doctrines, even proclaiming the name of Jesus or having the Holy Spirit, threaten the godly commitment of Christians. However, God's power is able to keep us from falling. But our responsibility is to build ourselves up in the truth of God's Word, pray in the Holy Spirit, and anticipate our final salvation (forever with Him and future blessings without any fruit of darkness).

The Scriptures are our resource. At the same time, we are to be alert, watchful, and vocal in warning those who are being swayed by false, humanistic philosophy—even at the risk of offending those close to you. God will have vengeance on all ungodly people as well as the angels that left their abode with Him to follow Satan. They will be condemned to eternal fire (v. 5-7). His vengeance is for rejecting or denying the only Lord, Jesus. For they turned the grace of the Lord Jesus into perversion (carnal, depraved, impure).

In contrast to false teachers who are devoid of the Spirit, it is important to realize the Holy Spirit is the One whom God uses to preserve His own from worldly error. Now to God, our Savior, who *alone* is wise, be glory and majesty, dominion and power both now and forever more (v. 25). God is amazing grace! God lavishes His love on His own. We can trust Him to impact every aspect of our life!

The Holy Spirit causes the Scripture to come alive and minister to each of us, to transform us into the likeness of Christ by producing the fruit and gifts of the Spirit. Our Christ-likeness is in His righteousness and holiness (Ephesians 4:22-24). Inner healing and physical healing, deliverance, peace and joy, and even becoming better persons are all by-products of knowing God and believing in Jesus' finished work on the Cross. Jesus said it was finished, and it is! These benefits come only by not being conformed by the standards or teaching of the world, but by being transformed by renewing our minds in the knowledge of God through His Word and praying in the Holy Spirit.

The Truth, Nothing But the Truth

God is awesome! Through His Spirit and His Word, He is transforming His character in us by the renewing of our mind because He is in us. No one or nothing else is needed—no program, self-help book, and no man! Do not let Christian psychology or spiritual psychology of any kind of mixture enter your mind—spend your time in God's Word and praying in the Spirit! Even Christian psychology or spirituality is Satan's attempt to capture your soul and cause you to surrender it to him. Even in exercises such as Christian yoga, your participation is giving consent to the invitation to enter into the spiritual philosophy and spirit behind it. By the way, "yoga" doesn't mean just "yoked to," it means in union with! The Hindu doctrine means to bow to the God within you (Brown, 2013). In union to what and to whom? The union of your mind and body with a demon spirit. That is not the promised Holy Spirit. You can't just sanctify another doctrine by adding "Christian" to it or plugging Jesus in. God clearly states that it is an abomination.

By mere participating, one has given permission for the demonic spirit behind the false religious philosophy to be activated in your life. You accepted the invitation! Guard your soul! Your responsibility is to establish absolute truth and put spiritual boundaries around yourself. The Holy Spirit cannot be separated from the doctrine of Jesus Christ. He is the Teacher, the Counselor, the Comforter, and the Enforcer of God's Word. He is the only way, only truth, and only life!

God makes it clear from the beginning when Joshua blessed the people one last time. In Joshua 23 and 24, he reminded them of God's warnings to fear the Lord, serve Him in sincerity and in truth; to put away the gods which their ancestors served as well as the gods in the land in which they were dwelling. God warns them that if they forsake the Lord to serve foreign gods, they would quickly perish in the land God promised them. As clearly as can be, God charged them with the words, "Choose for yourselves this day whom you will serve."

Our greatest challenge is our own perception of reality. Believe in Jesus. Believe that He is who He says He is and that He has a plan for you and a purpose to fulfill with your life. Cry out to Jesus—the Holy Spirit will bear witness in your spirit and you will know He is truth.

My Dad Said So
- I have been chosen by God (John 15:16).
- God Himself dances over me with singing (Zeph. 3:17).
- I am a bearer of good news (Isaiah 52:7).
- I have been sanctified and made truly holy (1 Cor. 6:11).
- I am always on God's mind, He thinks about me constantly (Ps. 139:17-18).
- Even before the creation of the world, I was planned (Eph. 1:4).
- I am a child of the King, adopted into his family! (Eph. 1:5).
- I am accepted in the Beloved (Eph. 1:6).
- I am an heir in Christ (Rom. 8:17).
- I am blessed with every spiritual blessing in heavenly places (Eph. 1:3).
- I am the righteousness of Christ (2 Cor. 5:21).
- I am a temple of the Holy Spirit (1 Cor. 6:19).
- I have an anointing from the Holy One and I know all things (1 John 2:27).
- I lack no good thing (Ps. 34:10).
- I am placed and seated with Him, a king and priest, part of a chosen generation, a peculiar people (1 Pet. 2:9).

- No weapon formed against me can prosper (Is. 54:17).
- No plague can come near my dwelling, my house, or my body (Ps. 91:10).
- My life was bought at a price. Jesus covered it (1 Cor. 6:20).
- My days are appointed (Ps. 139:16).
- My life is protected (Mark 16:18).
- Angels encamp around me (Ps. 34:7).
- The blessings of God encircle me (Ps. 103:4).
- Blessings go before me and overtake me (Deut. 28:2).
- The Creator of the universe, my Father (Abba—Daddy!) loves me with an everlasting love (Jer. 31:3).

God loves His kids! Wow! We are extraordinary Kingdom kids—Dad said so! Now activate your faith, another fruit God has already given you, by sharing and acknowledging all the good things He has given you.

...that the sharing of your faith may become effective by the acknowledgement of every good thing which is in you in Christ Jesus (Philemon 6).

Back to the Question: Where Do You Find Yourself?

Some of you love Jesus with all your heart, but you are not living the fruitful fullness of God in your life as God said we would. First, examine your heart and question whether or not you are you really born again and in a right relationship with Jesus. Many are living in sin but claim to be Christians and even claim they hear from God. The Holy Spirit's voice will never contradict God's Word—Never! For example, if you feel that it is okay to live a homosexual lifestyle or to live with someone outside of marriage, you are wrong. This is not the Holy Spirit speaking to you because

He will never contradict God's Word, even if you perceive God is telling you that it is okay. Call sin what it is, *sin*.

That being said, secondly ask the Holy Spirit to examine your heart and judge your life according to God's standards—are you really born again? If there is any doubt, call out to Jesus and let Him know you want Him to be Lord of your life. I refer you to Chapter 11—"Inspecting Your Foundation" for a thorough teaching on what it means to be a born-again, spirit filled, and fully devoted follower of Jesus Christ.

If you are reading this, and yes, you are disciple of Jesus, but you have entertained, participated in, or yoked yourself to anything that has been described previously in this teaching that is not of God, *repent and get rid of it and commit to make Jesus Lord!* As long as the Lord tarries, there is good news! There is not a formula, or recital, it is a person, Jesus!

REPENT
ASK Jesus to forgive you for _____ (whatever it is you have been embracing as truth, or an activity/participation contrary to the Word of God). Commit to make Him Lord, follow Him, and trust and obey His Word.

RENOUNCE the practice in Jesus' name.
Totally turn away from the practice.

COMMAND the anti-Christ spirits that had invitation to be there to leave *now*, in the name of Jesus.

RENEW
Embrace the truth and walk in the newness of your revelation of Jesus Christ.
Colossians 3:1-4 describes it well.

If then you have been raised with Christ, seek the things that are above, where Christ is, seated at the right hand of God. Set your minds on things that are above, not on things that are on earth. For you have died, and your life is hidden with Christ in God. When Christ who is your life appears, then you also will appear with him in glory.

REJOICE in what Jesus has done.

In place of what you just renounced, release truth and holiness in your life by speaking God's words out loud over your life. Give thanks to Jesus for His grace, mercy, and love towards you. Now activate your faith—you are free! Walk in the new revelation of who you are in Christ.

I thank my God, making mention of you always in my prayers, hearing of your love and faith which you have toward the Lord Jesus and toward all the saints, that the sharing of your faith may become effective by the acknowledgement of every good thing which is in you in Christ Jesus (Philemon 4-6 NKJV).

Sample Prayer

Lord Jesus I choose You! I renounce and I reject any current or previous connections to _____ (whatever it is you have been embracing as truth, or an activity/participation contrary to the Word of God). I break any covenants, any vows, any agreements, and any attachments I have made or have been made over my family either in ignorance or purposefully, in the name of Jesus.

In the name of Jesus, I break off any anti-Christ spirits, such as divination, witchcraft, whoredom, and error in which I have participated. I command these spirits, and anything that came with them, to leave now and to go to where Jesus would send them. In Jesus' name, I speak truth, holiness, and freedom over me and my family and future generations. In Jesus' name, I apply the Blood of Jesus over myself and my family.

Thank You, Lord Jesus, for Your grace, mercy, and love for me. I choose to make You Lord of my life. Holy Spirit, I ask You to fill me up with Your Spirit and line me up with the truth of God's Word. I trust You to direct my steps. In Jesus' name, amen!

Above All Else, Guard Your Heart— Free People Free People

Above all else, guard your heart, for it is the wellspring of life (Proverbs 4:23).

Spiritual health directly impacts physical health as well as eternal destiny. God wants us to walk in His Word, His Spirit, and from His heart! We have been hindered in growth, in blessing, and in unity because of heart conditions. We don't need to give the devil a platform in our lives. We just need to stay focused on Jesus. It is our heart conditions that cause stress and lead us to embrace another Jesus. All of our issues are heart issues—all of them!

Jesus wants to heal and restore our heart conditions. He is our Healer.

Conditions of the Heart:

1. **Rebellious Heart** - stubbornness, self-centeredness, disobedient, provoking turmoil and strife, bitter or unpleasant.

For rebellion is as the sin of witchcraft, and stubbornness is as iniquity and idolatry. Because thou hast rejected the word of the Lord, he hath also rejected then from being King. And Saul said unto Samuel, I have sinned, for I have transgressed the commandment of the Lord, and thy words: because I feared the people and obeyed their voice (1 Samuel 15:23 NKJV).

2. **Distracted or Divided Heart** - taking counsel in other things besides God—believing lies of the enemy instead of God's Word, doubt and fear.

Spiritual Psychology: Your Invitation to the Occult

Second Kings 1:1-18 (NKJV) is a story about King Ahaziah. He sent messengers to inquire of Baal-Zebub, the god of Ekron to see whether or not he would recover. An angel of the Lord told Elijah to intercept the messenger—and the messenger turned back. The king sent captains with multiple men—Elijah called fire from heaven to consume them. The king then inquired of Elijah, but Elijah said since he had sent messengers to inquire of Baal-Zebub, he would surely die.

3. **Fragmented or Wounded Heart**—victims of loss, trauma or abuse—unhealthy self-esteem, fearful, hiding behind a mask, relationship issues—often hurt people or are hurt by people. Hopelessness, suicide ideation.

Let God's revelation of who He is, who you are to Him, and all the good things He has given you now and your future destiny, overtake your past—so that you can become who God created and REDEEMED you to be. Jesus came to heal the broken hearted. While other philosophies promise, only Jesus can put the shattered, fragmented heart back together and brand new. You are not a product of your past or your circumstances; you are a product of the finished work of Jesus on the Cross! You have a new heart and a new life!

Jesus was wounded for our transgressions and He was bruised for our inequities; the chastisement for our peace was upon Him, and by His stripes we are healed (Isaiah 53:5 NKJV).

Then Jesus said to those Jews who believed Him, 'If you abide in My Word, you are My disciples indeed. And you shall know the truth and the truth shall make you free (John 8:31-32 NKJV).

There is now no condemnation to those who are in Christ Jesus, who do not walk according to the flesh, but according to the Spirit (Romans 8:1 NKJV).

For those who live according to the flesh set their minds on the things of the flesh, but those who live according to the Spirit, the things of the

Spirit. For to be carnally minded (the five senses/flesh) is death, but to be spiritually minded is life and peace. Because the carnal mind is enmity against God; for it is not subject to the law of God, nor indeed can it be. So then, those who are in the flesh cannot please God. But you are not in the flesh, but in the Spirit of God, if indeed the Spirit of God dwells in you. Now if anyone does not have the Spirit of Christ, he is not His. And if Christ is in you, the body is dead because of sin, but the Spirit is life because of righteousness (Romans 8:5-10).

Live Him and Lead by Living

The only answer to our world is the love and power of Jesus through us. Free people free people. The world, and even the church, tell us how to live; the world needs to see us live through Jesus Christ! We are to make disciples, not leaders, not programs. Our job is to live Him and then lead by living Him! He will be expressed through us. Then I can stand in awe of His majestic works and give Him all the glory and honor and praise. Believe that God will fulfill His plan through you as you surrender your life to Him. God is good!

In this the love of God was manifested toward us, that God has sent His only begotten Son into the world, that we might live through Him (1 John 4:9).

References

Yungen, R. (2006) *God in All Things? The Premise of Contemplative Spirituality Lighthouse Trails Research Project.* Lighthouse Trails Publishing, Inc. https://www.lighthousetrailsresearch.com/godinall-byray.htm

Heuertz, Christopher L. (2017). *The Sacred Enneagram: Finding Your Unique Path to Spiritual Growth.* Grand Rapids: Zondervan.

Pacwa, M. (2009) *Tell Me Who I Am, O Enneagram.* Article ID: DN067 Christian Research Journal. https://www.equip.org/article/tell-me-who-i-am-o-enneagram/

Smith, J. *What is Yoga?* https://www.truthbehindyouga.com/what-is-meditation/ (accessed 12/9/18)

6

Heart Intelligence

Emotional Intelligence, aka Heart-based Living, aka Intuitive Guidance, aka Psychophysiological Coherence, aka Neurocentricity, aka Contemplative Meditation or Mindfulness, aka Metaphysics, aka Global Coherence Initiative, aka Human Potential Movement, aka Integrative Medicine

Throughout the ages and across cultures, the heart has been considered a primary source of emotion, courage, and wisdom, and it's vital to sustain human life. Today, everyone is talking about the heart as if it were the true center of all wisdom. We hear phrases such as "follow your heart," "lead from your heart," "speak from the heart," "what does your heart say?" and of course, "it feels right."

While it is the nature of people to desire to learn and grow, today our culture is saturated with resources talking about the heart as being necessary for personal transformation and our intuitive (spiritual) guidance (divine compass) to become our true self of love and compassion. It is alarming that many professing Christians do not recognize the satanic spiritual philosophy behind these resources, techniques, and practices that are being used for stress management, and personal growth. Using science, psychology, and contemporary language of ancient Eastern mysticism and esoteric experiences, ancient pagan (demonic) "wisdom" and spirituality is repackaged as Heart-based Living or Heart Intelligence or Mindfulness.

Society is full of academicians and celebrities promoting themselves as the authority on optimizing human performance, personal effectiveness, and spiritual maturity. Heart Intelligence is a conceptual framework within the vast philosophies and doctrines of the New Age traditions of Eastern religions. Heart-based tools and meditation technologies are designed to connect you with your heart's intuitive guidance (spirit, energy, life force) so that you can learn to listen and follow your heart to fulfill your purpose, make better decisions, and be successful in life. In other words, the brain thinks, but the heart knows and gives direction.

Peter Shepherd (2018), one of the many teachers of Heart Intelligence, describes human beings as needing to be awakened to the soul that inhabits each body and is our true self and inner knowing. He further purports that humans need to become mindfully conscious instead of ruled by our instincts, past habits, or fixed beliefs—throwing away dogma and open our minds—to create our own reality by moving towards light or darkness. He describes God as the sum of all consciousness, encompassing both our light and our darkness; and our earth experiences are mainly the opportunity to decide which way we want to create. In addition, our higher self, the all-knowing part of us connected to all consciousness, communicates to our body-mind through the heart, not verbal messages; therefore, we must be open to receive this intuitive wisdom. Open to whom?

Intent Is Irrelevant

It is important that you get a glimpse of the teaching and doctrines behind the programs, techniques, and tools that are so prominent in our healthcare organizations, business practices ,and personal use for stress relief, relaxation, employee engagement and retention, and even in mainstream Christian churches for spiritual maturity. The next time you are asked to take a personality assessment, use a heart rhythm coherence monitor, participate in an emotional self-regulating technique, or engage in contemplative mediation or a mindfulness exercise in a coaching class, beware of what you are spiritually consenting to do by your mere participation. Discern the tools and symbols and meaning behind the tools such as the sacred Enneagram or the Target of Life. It is well documented that intent is irrelevant. Participation or practice in it without understanding the philosophy has negative outcomes because the spirit or deity behind the practice will begin to influence your belief system, as well as inhabit places in your life because you invited in the spiritual realm of darkness.

Heart Intelligence within this non-biblical context makes sense to a non-Christian. However to a Christian, it is deception because this describes a tangible awareness and esoteric energy (demonic) experience within someone to integrate the physical, mental, emotional, and spiritual components of a human being. The spiritual component in this philosophy connects the person to the "Greater Intelligence system" that is called many names, such as God, Spirit, the Universe, the Great Spirit, and even Life. This spirit is not Jesus Christ. The euphoric feelings of peace and love that people experience is not the Jesus Christ of the Bible.

Is This the Leader You Want to Follow?

As it goes, "Follow Your Heart" is a statement of faith and a gospel proclaimed by many. Essentially, it is a belief that your heart is a compass inside you that is your true guide to happiness if you have the courage to listen and follow it. Our heart will not save us. We need to be saved from our hearts.

The Follow Your Heart creed is not biblical. The Bible actually says our hearts are sick and deceitful. "The heart is deceitful above all things, and desperately sick: who can understand it?" (Jeremiah 17:9). In Matthew 15:19, Jesus lists the things that come out of it—"out of the heart comes evil thoughts, murder, adultery, sexual immorality, theft, false witness, slander, blasphemy." The truth is no one lies to us more than our own hearts! Our heart does not tell us the truth, and we want to use it as compass? Our heart is selfish and will consume everything for our own desires and self-indulgence. We open our heart to lies and people speaking apostasy to guide us. Jesus gave His life to save our heart (John 3:16) and lead our heart to exceeding joy (Psalm 43:4).

Don't follow your heart—follow Jesus! Jesus Himself said, "Don't let your hearts be troubled, believe in God; believe also in Me" (John 14:1). He didn't say believe in your heart but in Him! Jesus is the Shepherd, not our heart. Our heart tells us what we want but doesn't tell us where to go. The heart intuitive or spirit guidance that is being promoted or experienced in these spiritual techniques and philosophies is clearly demonic spirits instructing out of the heart. Our heart was never designed to be followed but to be led. Our hearts were never designed to be gods in whom we believe; we were designed to believe God.

Jesus said to follow Him—listen to His voice and follow Him (John 10:11.27). He is Truth and the Way, and will lead you to Life (John 14:6)

The Bible is clear that we do not wrestle against the flesh, but spirits and principalities.

For we wrestle not against flesh and blood, but against principalities, against powers, against the rules of the darkness of this world, against spiritual wickedness in high places. Wherefore take unto you the whole armor of God that ye may be able to withstand in the evil day, and having done all, to stand (Ephesians 6:12-13 KJV).

There are numerous tools and techniques, but as discussed before, know the source and type of treatment in which you are consenting. Heart Intelligence, as with many of the metaphysical, spiritual psychology, psychophysiology, alternative medicine and wellness initiatives, have common hidden philosophies for the West. The philosophy will encompass psychological, historical, social, spiritual, and mystical insights or ways to grow deeper in search for the meaning of life or spiritual awakening.

There is consciousness realization that the universe is living and that all is conscious and a dynamic energy (spirit, life force), including ourselves; we are all connected with each other as co-creators. There is a belief in Oneness when you connect with the divine energy (spirit, energy, life force) within yourself. You become empowered, and this mystical experience is thought to be key to overcoming conflict.

Lastly, meditation techniques are used and promoted as a way for us to become steady and constant in the present so that one can perceive that stress is self-imposed and the result of misconceived ideas and past beliefs. Through the contemplation and meditation of focusing on something, one begins to feel, see, and know things from their inner self. Many will use the term "when the spirit speaks," meaning your intuitive knowingness moves you. Do you see that if it is not Jesus, then it is another spirit guide instructing you? If it is not Jesus, it is a demon!

What Is Meditation?

A resource for anyone seeking truth about health and wellness practices using meditation or contemplative mindfulness techniques is www.truthbehindyoga.com. Author and fitness instructor Jessica Smith shares her testimony of how God rescued her from terrifying death grips that Satan had over her through Yoga and Reiki practices. Jessica was raised with a Christian upbringing but in pursuit of exploring spiritual truth, became a certified Yoga instructor and Master level Reiki practitioner. She studied and practiced under several spiritual teachers in various Eastern religions, such as in a Buddhist Center, a meditation retreat center in South America, and an ashram in India. She teaches and warns Christians about the mysterious realm of energies (demon spirits) and the paranormal and intense things that happened while experiencing peace and tranquility. Praise God, He miraculously rescued her. There are many similar testimonies that I have personally encountered in ministering healing. Many people have been deceived that they are serving Jesus while participating with deities behind exercise, holistic spiritual retreat gatherings, and alternative health treatments. The experiences are real.

Smith (2015) clarifies the antithetical definitions of meditation that are being increasingly confused as the same term in today's society. It is important to be clear on definitions because one leads to biblical understanding and the other leads to pagan spiritualism. One practice is rooted in biblical meaning, and the other in Buddhism, Hinduism, and other New Age traditions. It is important that this misconception be cleared.

A Christian meditating would be reading His Bible, thinking on the words that were read. He would be praying and worshipping God as He read the Bible and spent time with the Lord sitting naturally, maybe at the table or in a chair. There would not be specific pose required or repetition of particular prayer or sound or movements, just natural talking with the Lord or sitting quietly enjoying the thoughts of applying the Word he just read to his own life. During the day, when things got stressful, words from the Bible would enter his mind to remind him to not be anxious for anything. He would thank the Lord for His assurance of never leaving or forsaking him. This is a picture of biblical meditation.

Another person sits cross-legged or in a predetermined prayer posture. His eyes are fixed—not noticing anything around him—just focusing on the stillness and the quietness of his soul, his feelings, and the present moment. His body may subtly rock back and forth very rhythmically. Sometimes he may make a repetitive sound or word or repeat a prayer several times. This little prayer, or sound invokes the deity or "energy" associated with the sound to help him deepen his practice. Other times, he may do yoga movements instead of sounds or prayers. Sometimes he may hold a picture of a spiritual teacher in his mind or gaze at a sacred symbol or tool. Once in a while he may inhale the fragrance of an essential oil or use a hallucinogenic drug to help "open" him to new energies (demon spirits) that can take him to reach very deep esoteric levels, clarity of mind, and even courage. Using these various ways, he may practice meditation, but the goal is the same: To obtain absolute knowledge and freedom by uniting with the divine consciousness. This is a picture of Eastern Meditation/ Mindfulness.

One Word, Two Meanings: Empty vs Fill
The Misconception of Open-Minded "Mindfulness"

These two such different practices are called by the same name, yet they are totally opposite in practice and what they represent.

If someone is sitting cross-legged, posed, and chanting on a hillside in the sun or in front of a Buddha statute, it would be obvious what kind of meditation he or she is involved in. The problem, according to Jessica Smith (2018), the beginning steps to this type of meditation is what we are seeing everywhere, promoted on talk-shows, celebrities, health care facilities, gym classes, business executives for stress management, and employee wellness programs. It is easy to promote and seduce by using stress management relief or relaxation with simple exercises such as focusing on the breath or holding an image of something that elicits peace.

Sometimes, so-called mindful meditation, emphasizes the focus on one's surroundings, a feeling, sensation, the rhythm of your heart beat, etc. It can be called "open-minded," emphasizing the focus practice that is to let go of all thoughts. They are both the same kind of practice; however, they are not the biblical kind. They are the introductory lessons of the pagan practice designed to open oneself up to receive the spiritual realm. These are not spiritually neutral paths, as is being promoted, but rather they are lies to attract more people. Participants are often not even told they are engaging in spiritually opening practices. In this case, sounds are not just vibrations, and movements are not just stretching, but they are real and specific deities.

Author and Associate Professor of Religion at Indiana University, Candy Gunther Brown, warns us in the context of alternative medicine, yoga, and other spiritually rooted practices. She concluded from her studies that over time, people who start off attracted to an alternative practice because there is a perceived health benefit start to embrace the religious ideas underneath these practices. In other words, they change their original religious beliefs (*Christianity Today*, November 2013).

Christians tend to believe that a person's intent is what determines what is religious. They don't realize that active participation changes their intent and beliefs.

The Lord's Instruction for Meditation Is Filling the Mind

The Lord's instruction regarding meditation is to always be filling the mind with thoughts of Him. Because we love the Lord so much we think about Him all the time. The goal is to strengthen us in our relationship with Jesus and encourage us to delight in Him and worship Him with our thoughts and quiet prayers all day long. We get real peace because the Word is Jesus and He is in us. Real peace is a person—the Prince of Peace.

Eastern/New Age Instruction: Meditation—Empty the Mind

The direct opposite to biblical meditation, Eastern or New Age traditions instruct people to empty their mind of thoughts and to open their mind to the spiritual realm and ultimately reach a state of merging and oneness with the ultimate consciousness, or what is called God. Participants are told they can find their True Self and God. Sometimes they are given prayer postures based on their personality or specific spiritual pathway.

According to former practitioner Jessica Smith, this approach is widely masked at retreat centers as a non-spiritual practice. It is another lie. The goal is to get people hooked on the peaceful tranquility and feelings of love affects so that they keep returning for something deeper. This is real and dangerous. The most popular instruction we hear is to sit quietly and focus on something like on the breath or heart beat or an object or a spiritual teacher. They are told to just plug in Jesus if you are a Christian. The pagan practice is instruction to let go of thoughts and empty the mind of emotions in an effort to become open to receive from the spiritual realm—energies, spirits, powers—and become one or commune with their idea of god. Energy and Spirit are used interchangeably within the spiritual practice, but the end result is the same.

Results begin with feelings of peace, then a state of euphoria, and deepens further the more one practices or unites with whatever is evoked. The peaceful sensations and experiences are not a physiological reaction to breathing or focusing, as promoted. It is a spiritual practice, and that state is the result of being affected by a spirit (demon).

Of course, breathing, relaxation, and stretching and even plants are natural and God-given; on their own, they are good. The tree in the garden was good. The problem occurs when we practice these things in context with a spiritual doctrine or philosophy that has another god or gospel. The feelings of love and peace, visions, power, esoteric experiences, and tranquility are deception. They are not the true peace and love that only Jesus can give. Anything else is counterfeit and the source is demonic. These practices are aimed to separate us from God—it is a slippery slope. Christians are attracted to packages promising health and wellness, improving oneself, or leadership development but are unwise to not unwrap the packages before participating.

The Word of God—Jesus Is Our Peace

Please ask Jesus to examine your heart and reveal to you His truth about any pagan practices or mixed philosophies in your life. Turn away—run away now. Please do not turn back to these pagan practices in search of learning, seeking peace, or because others are doing it and you see nothing wrong with them. God loves us so much, and He wants us to know Him intimately through our relationship with His Son, Jesus Christ. Turn to Jesus to find peace and joy, even when we don't agree or understand, it is through faith, not our feelings.

Throughout the Bible, God gives specific instructions ensuring that followers are set apart, that we are far away from anything resembling practices or allegiances of surrounding nations and cultures with other gods. God called it spiritual harlotry. He wasn't being mean; we are His treasured people to be sanctified, to be set apart for Him, not copycats of those who don't know Him. We are not to adapt or blend with pagan spiritual practices. God calls us to Himself.

> *For what do righteousness and wickedness have in common? Or what fellowship can light have with darkness? what agreement is there between the temple of God and idols? For we are the temple of the living God. As God said: 'I will live with them and walk among them, and I will be their God, and they will be my people. Therefore, come out from them and be separate, says the Lord* (2 Corinthians 6:14-17).

> *Be careful not to be ensnared by inquiring about their gods, saying, "How will these nations serve their gods, we will do the same"* (Deuteronomy 13:30).

> *Destroy completely all the places on the high mountains and on the hills and under every spreading tree where the nations you are dispossessing worship their gods…You must not worship the Lord your God in their way* (Deuteronomy 12:2-4).

> *But you have carefully followed my doctrine, manner of life, purpose, faith, longsuffering, love, perseverance, persecutions, afflictions, which happened to me at Antioch, at Iconium, at Lystra—what persecutions*

I endured. And out of them all the Lord delivered me. Yes, and all who desire to live godly in Christ Jesus will suffer persecution. But evil men and impostors will grow worse and worse, deceiving and being deceived. But you must continue in the things which you have learned and been assured of, knowing from whom you have learned them, and that from childhood you have known the Holy Scriptures, which are able to make you wise for salvation through faith which is in Christ Jesus. All Scripture is given by inspiration of God, and is profitable for doctrine, for reproof, for correction, for instruction in righteousness, that the man of God may be complete, thoroughly equipped for every good work (2 Timothy 3: 10-17 NKJV).

O Timothy! Guard what was committed to your trust, avoiding the profane and idle babblings and contradictions of what is falsely called knowledge—by professing it some have strayed concerning the faith. Grace be with you. Amen (1 Timothy 6:20-24 NKJV).

Today, My Daily Bread

When God miraculously rescued the Children of Israel out of Egypt, He led them into the wilderness. God provided for them; however, He was detailed in their journey to spiritual maturity. The Bible tells us in Exodus Chapters 13-14 that God tested them because they had to learn to really trust and obey Him. When He gave them their daily bread, He didn't let them store anything up for tomorrow so He could reinforce to them they could trust Him to provide again tomorrow. While in the desert wilderness, God provided:

- A clear path for them to follow (cloud and fire).
- Protection from everything!
- Provision day by day—He was enough.
- The power of His Presence—God was with them always.

We should have the awareness that we belong to an amazing, miracle-working Provider, Father God. He gives us today our daily bread. He gives us what we need moment by moment for each day. Through Jesus Christ, His grace and provision is all that I need for today. We are not promised tomorrow, so each day we trust Him and thank Him for that day. When I am asleep, He is working on my behalf, and I can see the glory of what my Father has done every day.

God has not changed. We can be confident and assured that as we go through the wildernesses and difficulties of life, we should know that He has given us a clear path, provision, healing, and protection. He never leaves us. Jesus is the only path, provision, protection, and sustainer of divine health—He is the Daily Bread! Consider making Philippians 4 one of your life chapters to understand His path. Each of us can truly live—anxious for nothing and in everything giving thanks as we make our requests known to God.

Unfortunately many people don't have His path, His protection, nor His Presence because they are following the wisdom of men rather than Jesus. In Jesus, every day, every moment, we can live in the Presence of the Almighty, miraculous, awesome God! This is what Jesus offers to everyone who believes Him and commits to follow Him as Lord and Savior.

The Person of Jesus Christ in my life is the living bread of heaven that has come down to earth to you and me. You can live in the power of His grace and His Presence today and know Jesus will be enough. We can lay our heads down at night and say, "Thank You, Jesus, Thank You, Jesus, that You stand guard over me and my home. Thank You, Jesus, that the things I am concerned about and need today, I have already in You. Thank You, Jesus, that You are with me now and will never leave me.

Humanity's Common Ground: Searching for Peace

We can look around and it doesn't matter what people group, religious tradition, political affiliation, or celebrity or financial status, people are desperately searching for peace. Romans 1 describes our world's current state of affairs. We have substituted intimacy with God for the comforts and wisdom of the world. It has cost us greatly!

It is not about solving social issues or having the right political person in office. It is not about taking prayer out of schools or redefining marriage. It is not about children being raised without father leaders or homes with violence and domestic abuse. It is not even about terrorism or the drug addiction epidemic. None of these things would be happening, if the Church—those professing to be Christians—really knew their God. You can't trust someone you don't know and believe in. You can't pray in faith if you don't know the will of God. Your faith communicated is not effective (Philemon 6) when you can't acknowledge what all God has given us through His Son, Jesus Christ.

If we are looking for peace today, we need to start with a person. Peace is not an idea or a solution for world affairs. God didn't send Jesus so that there would peace in the world. Jesus came so the world could have peace with God. The prophecy of Jesus was promised years before an angel appeared to the shepherds at His birth. A child will be born and will be called among other things, "Wonderful, Counselor, Mighty God, Everlasting Father and Prince of Peace" (Isaiah 9:6). Jesus is the Prince of Peace.

Before Jesus ascended into heaven, He appeared to His disciples and "breathed on them" telling them to receive the Holy Spirit, and He said to them, "Peace be to you" (John 20:19-21). To have peace, we must have the promised peace of God operational in our life. Experiencing any other feeling or kind of peace is counterfeit and not Jesus. Jesus gives us peace that passes all understanding, and the world can't give it to us (John 14:27). Many are being captivated and deceived by a false peace and tranquility found through demonic spirits disguised as angels of light or energy. It is important to know the real Jesus and it is important for one to recognize red flags present to keep you focused on Jesus.

The Holy Spirit will teach you all things and will remind you of everything that I said to you. Peace I leave with you, My peace I give to you. Don't let your heart be troubled; do not be afraid (John 14:26-27).

Jesus is offering His peace – the world cannot produce or offer this peace. He is saying whatever the world is telling you is not true; it is a lie. The world says:

- You can find your True Self and become one with the Universe and find peace.
- You can love God and love others better through sacred tools or self-regulation through mindfulness from ancient pagan traditions.
- You can re-create your reality and choose peace.
- You center yourself or accept and release all your negative feelings, and your intuitive guide will bring you to a state of peace.
- When you abandon your former beliefs as only illusion, you will find peace.
- Everyone is a child of God by birthright, so you can achieve a state of peace because God is Love.

NO! Jesus said the peace that He is offering is not like the world gives. Jesus, the Prince of Peace, the Son of God, who died and resurrected to give us peace with God, also gives us His peace to dwell inside of us and by which we can have peace with each other. Jesus—a person alive today—ascended into heaven so He can continue to offer Shalom Peace to you and to me, each in our own lives. Jesus is our peace.

Why is there such disconnect between what God has given us and professing Christians not walking in it? Counterfeit gospels make this a major point to entice young people to discard previous beliefs because it does not appear to be working. Yikes! People are straying away from God and find themselves depressed, anxious, suicidal, and addicted to substances to curb their pain or hopelessness. Something is terribly wrong!

Three things stand out. First, we are inundated with negativity and everything that is anti-Christ through instant media is instantly communicated all around us. Secondly, there is no off button or reprieve unless we are intentional about guarding our eyes, our minds, and our hearts.

Thirdly, and so tragic, Christians are entertained by and pursuing metaphysical philosophies (other gods) that promise something complementary or superior to the Word of God. These result in a person rejecting the doctrine of Christ because of unbelief or a building a faulty spiritual foundation stemming from wrong teaching. Both affect eternal destiny!

How Do We Get This Peace?

God has not changed. God is still speaking. He always speaks in the midst of our storms. He is still speaking His promises and leading us to His Words such as Philippians 4, from rejoicing always to God supplying all of our needs.

At some point, each person must take action to begin to follow Jesus—reading His Word, which is how we renew our minds and gain knowledge of Him and His instructions. The Word of God will transform you as the Holy Spirit teaches you and gives revelation. The world opposes and counterfeits God's instruction by promoting that our heart's intuitive guidance or intelligence will bring the ultimate knowledge and peace. The Holy Spirit will mature you and align you with the mind of Christ. In fact the mark of spiritual maturity and devotion for a Christ-follower is one recognized as having a wholehearted, focused pursuit of Jesus (Philippians 3:14-16).

Secondly, we must each take charge of our commitment to become a fully devoted disciple and follower of Jesus. To do that, you must lay down your life and pick up His. You have been bought with a price—the Blood of Jesus—so you now belong to Him and His ways and purpose for your life. Jesus must sit in the Captain's seat and not you nor any other gods. Surrender to Jesus and let Him lead you. Your life is His, and you live in Him and through Him, and Him alone!

Rejoice in the Lord always. Again I will say, rejoice! Let your gentleness be known to all men. The Lord is at hand. Be anxious for nothing, but in everything by prayer and supplication, with thanksgiving, let your requests be made known to God; and the peace of God, which surpasses all understanding, will guard your hearts and minds through Christ Jesus. Finally, brethren, whatever things are true, whatever things are noble, whatever things are just, whatever things are pure, whatever things are lovely, whatever things are of good report, if there is any virtue and if there is anything praiseworthy—meditate on these things. The things which you learned and received and heard and saw in me, these do, and the God of peace will be with you (Philippians 4:4-9).

There it is—be anxious for nothing, and praying with thanksgiving and petition about everything. And this peace that is bigger than our minds can comprehend is literally taking up a post guarding our minds and hearts in Christ Jesus! That means peace guards our emotions, and anything trying to get at our thoughts, emotions, and feelings will fail because we are guarded by the Prince of Peace! He said He would guard our hearts and minds because of our connection and relationship with Jesus Christ. That is the opportunity—the possibility that is authentic and real for each person who makes Jesus Lord! You have to activate this in your life. Each person must be spiritually born-again into Christ and make Him Lord of our lives.

Don't let anyone convince you that you have to attain it by going back to identify and connect with your past feelings, wounds, or events, and work through them. Don't let anyone convince you that you can find this peace by self-regulating your breathing or monitoring your emotions to live through your heart, or any other tool, posture, or mindful meditation technique or practice. God's peace surpasses all of man's wisdom and understanding.

If you are embracing God's truth that Jesus is all you need, and you are committed to making Jesus Christ Lord of your life, you will walk away from false doctrines and mixtures of Jesus and darkness or evil.

God has made it clear that we are not to have fellowship with darkness or practices that align themselves with the spirit realm of demons (spirit, energy, life-force). Be aware of the meaning of terminology used in psychophysiology practices. The power and peace is not a physiological response but a spiritual influence. Being fully devoted to following Jesus will protect your heart and mind because it is His peace.

The Holy Spirit will reveal truth to you as you read God's Word. As you are pursuing Jesus, if you have been believing a lie, then embrace the truth of God's Word, thank Him, and start walking in His truth. Don't let anyone manipulate your thoughts, your feelings, or your will by having you reflect on your past. Your past no longer defines you or should hold you in bondage.

Reset Your Concept of Jesus

Jesus is a multidimensional powerful personality who is alive and living in those that are His. Spend greater time in His Word and begin to see Him more than as just a historical picture in a cathedral or hologram superhero on a movie screen or in the pages of a story book. Caricatures or pictures won't help you when you get a diagnosis of cancer, a relationship dissolves, or you are without a job—things you didn't see coming and you can't control.

We need the Prince of Peace standing guard over our mind and heart! Jesus is a real personality moving through history. He was there when you derailed, not the psychologist. He is ahead of you in your thoughts and plans about tomorrow. He is intentional about showing up in the midst of our situations—we can expect Him! Praise God, He will never leave you and He still heals, delivers, and restores all things.

Jesus is real. He is tangible, He is mighty, and He's personable and knowable. This peace that guards the heart and guards the mind is Christ—He is the greatest person you will ever know in your life who is on board with everything that matters to you today. He promises to perfect that which concerns us (Psalm 138:8). He is coordinating history because He conquered the grave, and He is coming back to this planet to restore Shalom (peace) once and for all with a brand new heaven and earth. You can put your trust in Him!

Release Your Cares TO HIM!

You have to learn to release your cares to Jesus. You can only share your heart and release your concerns to someone you trust. How real is He to you? Is He as real to you as the person sitting next to you or even more real than that? If He is not as real as that, then you simply have an idol in your mind. You must have someone powerful and mighty like God in the Bible in your relationship, and then you can release your concerns to Him. You can only be anxious about nothing if you trust God with everything! You won't trust God with anything unless the person you are in relationship with is someone who can be trusted.

First Peter 5:7 (NKJV) says, "Cast all your anxieties on Him because He cares for you." Whatever is pulling your peace apart, your mind apart, your heart apart, cast it or place it on the very Person of Jesus Christ. Bring your cares to Jesus! He is the highest authority, the highest, most supreme commander; therefore, what He says is final. He told us to cast our cares on Him. Philippians 4 tells us that in every situation to make our requests known to God by prayer and thanksgiving.

Jesus is the King of Kings, who does miracles and makes things that are impossible become possible. He will make a way when there seems to be no way to change the circumstances. He will keep His Word!

You don't have to work through your issues alone—give them to God! You don't have to self-regulate your emotions or self-improve, nor do mindful meditation—give them to God! You don't have to numb yourself or chemically change your brain—just give the issues to God! If you have something making you anxious or fearful, take it to the very throne room of God, in Jesus' name!

Don't try to do things by yourself or fix things yourself. Don't look for alternatives or false teaching that directs you to look inward to find your True Self, or your Heart Intelligence, Intuitive Guidance, or your Being. These are demonic powers to try to copycat God but will lead you away from Him and eventually have you wanting to die yet promising peace. Don't take counsel or practice any other spirituality or worldview. Just give your issues and anxiety or fear to God, the King of the Universe, who you have constant access to through Jesus Christ. You let your requests be made known to the King of the Universe. Why would you want anyone else to champion your concerns and desires? Not me; not when I have the real deal and the most treasured relationship of all time!

We are not all one with the Universe as many teach. God is King of the Universe, and He creates all things and holds all things together. He is for us, not against us!

Thank Him for What He Has Done, Is Doing, and Will Do

God, the Almighty, your Abba (Daddy) Father is in charge and has authority over everything in the Universe, so we can take our concerns and requests directly to Him. What a privilege and honor to be His son or daughter through the sacrificial blood of Jesus so that we could have peace with God and have the Prince of Peace, also called Mighty and Counselor, guard our heart and our mind in Christ. He is praiseworthy and we respond with hearts of thanksgiving and gratitude for who He is and who we are to Him. By the way, "Counselor" in the Hebrew text such as Isaiah 9:6 doesn't mean a psychology or social work counselor that we use today. It meant a wise king who could be trusted. The prophetic word was describing Jesus!

You are His workmanship; you are fearfully and wonderfully made. He knows all about you and where you are going. He knows your needs before you ask and knows exactly how to perfect that which concerns you. You have direct access all the time. There is no one in the whole universe that cares about you more than He does.

Do you see why God said to have no other gods but Him? Do you understand why it is an abomination to God when people use mediums, postures, energy channeling, spirit guides, symbols, or spiritual pathways based on your personality? Trafficking in the spiritual realm is forbidden by God. He alone demands and deserves to be worshipped, loved, and honored. No other gods!

Can you see why the devil hates you? Satan will attempt anything to distract you away from God to place your affections on and express your worship to him rather than God. He will attempt to make you change your view and foundational beliefs about God and His criteria for salvation.

Jesus said, "narrow and difficult is the path and few find it" (Matthew 7:14). Is it because people are unwilling to give up their life for His or unwilling to pursue holiness and godliness because those things don't quite fit into our culture? People are unwilling to come out from the world and be separate. In other words, people are unwilling to make Jesus Lord and follow His Word and His ways. The question becomes, if we know this Prince of Peace, why wouldn't we?

> *My son, give attention to my words; Incline your ear to my sayings. Do not let them depart from your eyes; Keep them in the midst of your heart; For they are life to those who find them, And health to all their flesh. Keep your heart with all diligence, For out of it spring the issues of life. Put away from you a deceitful mouth, And put perverse lips far from you. Let your eyes look straight ahead, And your eyelids look right before you. Ponder the path of your feet, And let all your ways be established. Do not turn to the right or the left; Remove your foot from evil* (Proverbs 4:20-27 NKJV).

Treasure who you are in Christ and all that He has given you now and your destiny of eternal life one day with Him forever. Don't let anyone make you take your eyes off Jesus or wander away from your Shepherd. One night I was dreaming, and the Lord told me that the reason the eyes of a person wander is because there is a need to look other places for things a person perceives he doesn't already have. In other words, people are searching for things that can only be found in Christ and in Christ we have all things. He is enough! Do we really believe it?

> *His divine power has granted to us all things that pertain to life and godliness, through the knowledge of him who called us to his own glory and excellence* (2 Peter 1:3).

> *Blessed be the God and Father of our Lord Jesus Christ, who has blessed us with every spiritual blessing in the heavenly places in Christ* (Ephesians 1:3 NKJV).

Replace the Lies with the Truth of God

Replace the lies that have taken you away from God in deception. Replace the negative thoughts and feelings with renewing your mind on God's words and watch your feelings and emotions line up with His Word as evidenced by joy and peace. Think on things that are good and pure, praiseworthy and excellent. Meditate (biblical kind) on God's Word and do what He says. God promises His peace!

> *Finally, brethren, whatever things are true, whatever things are noble, whatever things are just, whatever things are pure, whatever things are lovely, whatever things are of good report, if there is any virtue and if there is anything praiseworthy—meditate on these things. The things which you learned and received and heard and saw in me, these do, and the God of peace will be with you* (Philippians 4: 8-9).

Repent and ask Jesus to forgive you for believing the lies; renounce the lies, and begin walking in your recommitment to God's truth.

Thank God for heavenly peace. Rest and sleep describe heavenly peace! Stay confident knowing God Himself is guarding over your house, your family, your business. God is working on our behalf even when we sleep. We can have sweet uninterrupted sleep when we have His peace. God has given every creature what they need, and He watches over them. Not one bird falls from the sky that isn't noticed by Him. God will give you exactly what you need from His perfect Father's heart. As we seek Him and delight in Him, He will even give you the desires of your heart (Psalm 37:4).

Put God first in everything. Pray only to Him, in Jesus' name. Just talk conversationally with Him. Reverence Him as the Mighty King of the Universe but love and honor Him as a good, good Father! We are hidden in Christ, and nothing can separate us from Him when we belong to Christ.

We guard our hearts and our minds by making Jesus Christ,

Lord—laying down our lives and picking up the Cross (His life). We separate ourselves from false teaching and evil practices. We ask God to choose our friends and leadership relationships. We let Him identify and then we remove anything in our lives that would hinder us from being fully devoted Disciples of Christ. Jesus (Prince of Peace) will also guard our heart and our mind through His peace, which cannot be harnessed or understood by this world. Through prayer and reading God's Word, we renew our minds and begin to know God more, and He transforms us and He produces fruit. We line up our words with His words because the words from our own mouths then produce fruit of life and death (Proverbs 18:21).

He is the vine, we are the branches (John 15:5). If we are connected to the vine, He produces the fruit. Satan is cursed and limited; however, he is powerful in the earth as he temporarily rules from the Kingdom of darkness. Because of Jesus in us, Satan is powerless for those who are hidden in Christ. The Prince of Peace Himself stands guard over our heart and mind.

> *I am the vine, you are the branches. He who abides in Me, and I in him, bears much fruit; for without Me you can do nothing. If anyone does not abide in Me, he is cast out as a branch and is withered; and they gather them and throw them into the fire, and they are burned. If you abide in Me, and My words abide in you, you will ask what you desire, and it shall be done for you. By this My Father is glorified, that you bear much fruit; so you will be My disciples* (John 15:5-8 NKJV).

As Christ's Ambassadors, we are charged to make disciples, preach the Word, heal the sick, and set the captives free.

Going Where No One Has Gone Before: Who Is at the Helm?

When searching for peace, we began with a prophecy declaring a person would be born who would be called "Wonderful, Counselor, and Prince of Peace." Let's look at what else the Old Testament prophet Isaiah said in Isaiah 9:6 (NKJV).

For unto us a Child is born,
Unto us a Son is given;
And the government will be upon His shoulder.
And His name will be called
Wonderful, Counselor, Mighty God,
Everlasting Father, Prince of Peace.

"And the government will be upon His shoulder" means that on Him will rest the entitlement to rule! Counselor, according to commentaries, expresses His ability as a political King and trusted leader. Paul's writings to the Romans confirms that peace comes from God and is evidence of the rule of Jesus, the Messiah—the Prince of Peace—who desires to reveal Himself and rule in each of our souls. We must choose Him.

Beloved of God, called to be saints: Grace to you and peace from God our Father and the Lord Jesus Christ (Romans 1:7 NKJV).

Just as the saving power of His death and resurrection makes it possible for us to have peace with God (being reconciled to Him), the indwelling of His life and character through the work of the Holy Spirit, teaches us to abide in the peace of God.

For I am not ashamed of the gospel of Christ, for it is the power of God to salvation for everyone who believes, for the Jew first and also for the Greek. For in it the righteousness of God is revealed from faith to faith; as it is written, "The just shall live by faith" (Romans 1:16-17 NKJV).

Therefore, having been justified by faith, we have peace with God through our Lord Jesus Christ, 2 through whom also we have access by faith into this grace in which we stand, and rejoice in hope of the glory of God (Romans 5:1-2 NKJV).

Mentioned earlier, before Jesus ascended into heaven, Jesus said to His disciples, "Peace I leave with you; My peace I give to you" (John 14:27). Surrendering your life to Him, His will, and His Word will bring inner rest and healing as we allow Jesus to rule in our hearts. His peace will rule over any anxiety or decision that would trouble you. His peace overrules any doubts that would disturb or distract you. And His peace will overthrow any lies of the devil attempting to deter or defeat you.

Wow, what a kingdom government in which we can live! Jesus is the living Word, the infallible source of guidance, the inexhaustible wisdom of God, the Truth, and the Way. On Him will rest this government. Perfect peace is available when the heart and mind are focused on God's promises, power, and presence with us. Trust Him!

You will keep him in perfect peace, Whose mind is stayed on You, Because he trusts in You (Isaiah 26:3 NKJV).

Why All the Fuss About the Heart? It Is All About the Heart!

Proverbs 4:20-23 tells us to guard our heart and keep God's words in the midst of our heart because life's issues flow out of it. All of the issues in our life are heart issues. All of them! Jesus wants our heart. Jesus wants our love, devotion, and worship. It shouldn't surprise you; how many people forget that Satan also wants your love, devotion, and worship.

What is worship? Worship is a lifestyle of our love expressed to God in response to His grace and mercy towards us. We know Satan, the deceiver, has already been defeated and judged, and will one day be cast into the lake of fire (Revelation 20:10); however, he is still vying to be worshipped.

We can only worship and trust things we love, and we express what we love. People don't have a problem expressing a pay raise or an answered prayer but have difficulty expressing the value of God's grace and mercy to save us. We can't worship, trust, or obey God if there is no love. We won't express our worship or obey God's Words if His love is not in our heart.

My son, give attention to my words; incline your ear to my sayings. Do not let them depart from your eyes; keep them in the midst of your heart; for they are life to those who find them, and health to all their flesh. Keep your heart with all diligence, for out of it spring the issues of life (Proverbs 4:20-23 NKJV).

What Does A Heart Look Like? Guard the Throne!

When one talks about the heart, the love of God, or even worship, we generally conceptualize many things. God makes the heart a topic of teaching way too many times for there to be room for confusion.

We know that we are triune beings. We have a spirit, a soul, and a body. The soul generally is described as our will, mind, and emotions. What is the heart other than an anatomical part of our body in the middle of our chest? The heart has been described throughout the ages in all worldviews in terms of descriptions our feelings, emotions, character, thoughts, the will, intellect, and conscience. In other words, the heart describes all the many facets of our soul. That is why pagan doctrines make the heart the power essence of the human being. It is with all these facets of the soul, we make decisions about what we love, trust, and worship. Do you see why Satan so desperately tries to capture your heart?

The best parable description that I have found that describes our heart is that of a command center or bridge of a ship. One pastor I heard recently used the visual of the command central bridge of a space ship in Star Trek. It really makes sense when you imagine that on a ship, there is only one Captain's seat and only one person qualified to sit in that seat. From this seat, all the operations of the entire ship originate, are implemented and coordinated, as well as evaluated. Only one!

When we talk about who is on the throne of your heart, believers agree that it should be Jesus. When we talk about Jesus being Commander and Chief, we are talking about Him being in the seat of ultimate authority and control. From this position or seat, He rules our hearts as the living Word, the infallible source of Wisdom, the Truth, the only Way, and Life. This seat was designed for only one, and God, through Jesus Christ, is supposed be sitting on the throne of your heart (the Captain's seat).

It is important to be intentional and aware of who sits on the throne of your heart. Who or what are you allowing to sit in the Captain's chair? If it is not Jesus, it is Satan disguised as light and other good things we desire, love, and worship. It is important, because from this chair or command center we call our heart, you begin to direct your thoughts, feelings, and emotions that result in decision making and thus experience the subsequent consequences in life. The problem, though, is that the consequence could determine where you spend your eternity. Who you allow to sit on the throne of your heart is a huge deal!

The problem for many of us, if we really took inventory of who or what was guiding our ship, something else is in the captain's seat. Christians believe they don't worship idols. You see, anything that takes the place of God on the throne of your heart and giving directions to you is an idol. God is clear about us not worshipping idols (other gods). It is important to let the Holy Spirit teach us and give us understanding in the details of our lives. God is personable and has our best interests on His heart. He wants us to succeed in what He has purposed us to be.

For I know the thoughts that I think toward you, says the LORD, thoughts of peace and not of evil, to give you a future and a hope (Jeremiah 29:11 NKJV).

What is happening in your life? Maybe He was on the throne of your heart but now the blessing is. For example, you got a new job and now work is on the throne, and you don't have time to read your Bible. Maybe a relationship or friends are on the throne of your heart and what they think or say directs your emotions, thoughts, and will, and your interests and time for God are different. Sitting on your throne could be your feelings, your family, or your ministry, such as church growth. What drives your emotions, thoughts, and actions? Children are blessings, but then we don't have time to spend with the Lord; He no longer the priority—the children take priority. The blessing replaced the God of the blessings. And we thank God for the things that replaced Him. We then wonder why things seem to go terribly wrong.

Other things from the heart that control our thoughts, emotions, and actions could be things such as worry and anxiety, fear, suicide ideation, guilt and shame, exercise and dieting, and not just activities such as sports and people such as celebrities. These things all affect our conscious thinking, emotions, and feelings, which in turn affect our will or decisions.

What is sitting on the throne of your heart controls you, directs you, gives you instructions, and has the final say. All your issues are heart issues! Salvation is a heart issue. That is why God wants your heart. As the Prince of Peace, He will stand guard over your heart and your mind, and He will direct your thoughts which will, in turn, line up your emotions and actions with His Word and presence. He will do it if we make Him Lord of our heart.

Proverbs 23:7 says, "For as a man thinks in his heart so is he." It doesn't say *what* He thinks but *as* he thinks. It is vital that we have God's perspective, His instructions, and His blessings. If you don't put God back in His rightful place, you will not have the life He intended for you to have.

God only wants our heart! God wants to change our heart because our actions, our trust, and our worship come out of the heart.

The world is trying everything to change one's thoughts to then change feelings, and then subsequent behavior will change.

Jesus says in Matthew 15:19 that evil comes from our hearts. That is why we end up doing things we regret or didn't think through because many act on what feels right instead of what was best. It is essential that God be the only one that sits on the throne of our heart. He will change our heart to produce fruit that bears life and brings Him glory. We choose our source of life by choosing who sits on the throne of our heart. That is why a relationship with Jesus is better than anything that you could ever have. Only God knows where you are going and how to get you there.

God sees through all of time, and His plans for us are good! He knows the plans He has for us for our hope and future. He is the only one to trust with our heart! I am pleading with you to watch the throne of your life!

God is the only one worthy to be praised and trusted, and the only one qualified to sit on the throne of your heart. He paid the price and He is the only one who has gone through everything necessary to take the helm of your life. Trust Him!

Everything else is counterfeit. Nothing or no one can provide for you what God can and has already provided for you. It is crucial that you make sure that Christ and He alone is on the throne of your heart. An idol is anything that replaces Him. God will allow things to fall through that were once considered blessings if we continue to ignore His instructions. The whole theme of the Scriptures is worship God, trust and obey Him, and Him alone.

Come Out of Egypt

God made application to us by the examples of the children of Israel. They lacked faith in God and made foreign alliances that they thought would help them or protect them from death. One prominent ally was Egypt who became a refuge of lies and harm. Commentaries report that they knowingly flirted with evil. Egypt represents you without God, bound in sin or deception. That is a scary place to be when one knowingly brings in other things alongside your worship and service to God.

God prohibits serving Him and idols together. He is clear about serving Him—worshipping Him and only Him through our relationship with Jesus.

Idols hinder your relationship and growth with God. We were all created to worship, and we will each naturally worship something or someone. Who or what is your source of life?

Second Kings 17 records specific instructions to the children of Israel. God brought them out of a brokenness type of situation and into a promised land. Even though they had a covenant with God, they began following after pagan practices that God specifically charged them to not do (verse16). Verse 17 records that they practiced witchcraft and soothsaying and sold themselves to do evil in the sight of the Lord, which provoked Him to anger. While still worshiping God (verse 33), people feared the Lord yet served their own gods. This resulted in syncretism (merging of different beliefs and practices).

They tried to worship God with other things at the same time. God said because they were mixing, He allowed the King of Assyria to come in and take them out of the Promised Land. It didn't work then; it won't now. Just in this chapter alone, God told them over and over not to serve or bow down or fear other gods, but to this day they do not fear the Lord nor do they follow His statutes or instructions (verse 34).

In 2 Kings 17:36-41, God charged them to worship only the Lord who brought them out of Egypt. He tells them not to forget and have no other gods before Him, or serve no other gods. He did not want to be worshipped with any other gods, period. Sadly, in verse 40, people would not listen and continued to follow their former practices. They thought they were good, and even more tragic (verse 41), their descendants to this day are doing the same.

Who are these descendants? Is it us? Sadly, yes, for me it was until the Lord identified that I began to put my career at the center of my heart. I am thankful that God got my attention; it was clearly not okay. His promises are true. He says if we put Him at the center of our hearts, He will direct our steps. We will get to the career to which He has called us if He is on the throne of our heart.

If we do not understand this, we will function in a delusion that it is okay to have anyone or anything in the captain's seat directing or speaking into your life. When God is not on the throne of your heart, it is hard to believe or trust Him and receive from Him. If God is not on the throne, it is hard to worship Him and know what He is calling you to do. Idols hinder your growth and relationship with Jesus.

A common delusion that is surfacing through these heart living and wisdom intelligence tools and techniques for stress relief or performance improvement is the inward reflection to self. Contemplative meditation or mindfulness asks you to be open and vulnerable to receive. These again are dangerous because you are inviting other entities, as well as your own feelings and thoughts, to be your focus, which in turn opens the spiritual realm of darkness to you—the exact things God sternly and repeatedly warned His children not to do. It breaks His heart!

God, through your relationship with Jesus Christ, is the only rightful person to be on the throne of your heart. Please don't miss this. Red flags should be going up all over the place for you when someone tells you to be open or vulnerable. Red flags should be there when you are using tools from pagan religions or ancient wisdom tools or authors from New Age and religious traditions that don't believe Jesus is the Son of God and that you have to be born-again. The red flags are there—please don't ignore them. The unction from the Holy Spirit is there—don't ignore Him like the children of Israel did. Jesus came to destroy the works of the devil and we do not have to repeat their mistakes.

Things that penetrate your heart begin to distract, counterfeit, and kick God out of His rightful place. The counterfeit things will mess with your mind, feelings, emotions, and thoughts. If the source is not the kingdom of God, then it is demonic. There are no neutral zones. When you open your heart to anyone but Jesus, you open doors, or give consent, to the demonic realm.

People are frivolous in opening their hearts to everyone and everything without realizing the impact of what is penetrating the heart and affecting emotions, belief systems, and the mind. Social media opens your heart to everyone. Look at your music. You may like the artist or the beat of a song, but the words are penetrating your heart. Consider the people to whom we listen and from whom we are taking advice—prescribing information for our health and well-being, and teaching us a false gospel. Everything impacts our heart. Guard it. Ask the Lord to make whatever adjustments need to be made in your life to protect your heart and align your will, mind, and emotions with His Word.

We have a decision right then. Say no—cast down every vain imagination that would exalt itself against the knowledge of God (the Captain of my ship). Say "'Get out. I command you to leave in Jesus' name! You can't stay! I have to renew my mind by getting into the Word of God." The Word of God (Jesus) will transform you from the inside out. Reading the Bible is not optional. Being part of a community (not merely attending church) is not optional. If you are not doing these things, you are not guarding your heart. You will continually be ransacked, persuaded, and tormented by anyone and anything that can get into the captain's seat. It is not until Someone with authority can tell you who you are and begins to push back the darkness and get back onto the throne of your heart. The only One that can do it, is Jesus.

Proverbs 4:23 says, "above all else" to guard your heart . No explanation is needed! The direction of your life is impacted by your heart. God wants you to re-present Him as His ambassador in areas of influence to which you are called. He must be on the throne and the One leading to do it. It all comes back to Jesus.

If there is an area of your life where you know something or someone else has been on the throne of your heart, pray now. God will show you things and dethrone those things in the name of Jesus and invite Jesus back to His rightful place.

PRAYER

Father, I thank you today that you examine the hearts of your children and are making adjustments right now. Father God, right now begin to change me from the inside out. I thank You, Father, that the things that have been on the throne of my heart—material things, relationships, emotions, or following wrong teaching—and anything else You show me, must be dethroned and come off right now in Jesus' name. I declare today that the throne of my heart is reserved for only You, Jesus, my Savior and Lord, none other. Jesus, I thank You for saving me, healing me, and setting me free to walk fully in Your love and power. I trust You, Lord to transform me into a fully devoted disciple. I surrender my life to You, Jesus. Make any adjustments that need to be made to protect my heart. I love You, Lord with all my heart. In Jesus' name, amen.

My son, give attention to my words; Incline your ear to my sayings. Do not let them depart from your eyes; keep them in the midst of your heart; for they are life to those who find them, and health to all their flesh. Keep your heart with all diligence, For out of it spring the issues of life. Put away from you a deceitful mouth, And put perverse lips far from you. Let your eyes look straight ahead, And your eyelids look right before you. Ponder the path of your feet, And let all your ways be established. Do not turn to the right or the left; Remove your foot from evil (Proverbs 4:20-27 NKJV).

References

Shepherd, P. *Heart Intelligence: Tools for Transformation.* Free E-book distributed by TRANS4MIND.COM. https://trans4mind.com/heart/Heart.pdf (Accessed on 12/02/18).

Smith, J. www.truthbehindyoga.org *But My Yoga Class... Addressing "Christian Yoga" and "Yoga for Exercise Only"* (Accessed on 12/09/18).

Smith, J. https://www.truthbehindyouga.com/what-is-meditation/*What Is Yoga?* (Accessed on 12/09/18).

Rozeman, D. (2017) https://www.huffingtonpost.com/entry/mindfulness_b_2980134 Wisdom 2.0: *The Rise of Compassionate Mindfulness =Heartfulness* (Accessed 12/02/18).

Gonsalves, G. (2018) https://www.heartintelligencecoach.com/what-is-heartintelligence/ *What Is Heart Intelligence?* (Accessed 12/02/18).

McCraty, R., Deyhle, A., & Childre, D. Global Advances in Health and Medicine. 2012 Mar; 1(1):64-77. https://www.ncbi.nlm.nih.gov/pmc/articles/PMC3833489 *The Global Coherence Initiative: Creating a Coherent Planetary Standing Wave* (Accessed 12/02/18).

Universe of Possibilities: Heart Intelligence. University of Kentucky, Module #4 of 10. *Skills for Creating Happiness and Blessing Others.* http://www2.ca.uky.edu/HES/fcs/possibilities1/Final_Publications/No4--Heart_Intelligence--DM.pdf (Accessed 12/02/18).

Christianity Today (2013). What Christians Need to Know about Alternative Medicine. November 2013, 57(9). https://www.christianitytoday.com/ct/2013/november/nonchristian-roots-alternative-medicine-candy-gunther-brown.html (Accessed on 12/29/18).

Gunter Brown, C. (2013). *The Healing Gods: Complementary and Alternative Medicine in Christian America.* New York: Oxford University Press.

7

Pharaoh Has Been Challenged: Are You Desperate Yet?

The *pharaonic* anti-Christ spirit is here and declaring itself as god—but make no mistake, it has been challenged!

This is the exultant city that lived securely, that said in her heart, "I am and there is no one else." What a desolation she has become, a lair, for wild beasts! Everyone who passes by her hisses and shakes his fist (Zephaniah 2:15).

Woe to her who is rebellious and defiled, the oppressing city! She listens to no voice; she accepts no correction. She does not trust in the Lord; she does not draw near her God (Zephaniah 3:1-2).

Anti-Christ spirits are holding on to power, authority, wealth, and knowledge at the deadly expense of the masses serving them. For decades there has been reported deception and fraud in the governance and practice of health and related organizations such as pharmacy and psychology. People continue to mock God's Word and His creation by the manipulation of the elements of the earth and the created species. What was once used to discover the marvels and majesty of God's glory is being used to harm people and turn good to evil. Is it a coincidence that in Egyptian times, this was considered sorcery? Is it coincidence that the root word of pharmacy means witchcraft and sorcery? The Bible calls this manipulation witchcraft.

Today, there are scientists and medical professionals trying to sound alarms, using real evidenced based research. They are challenging widespread ethical principles and practices within major national and world funding and policy making organizations. These organizations are being accused of manipulating and suppressing data that show that healthy people, through drugs and vaccines, are being made chronically ill and disabled. They are challenging that these organizations are not just manipulating data but also redefining terminology to spin results and promote false rhetoric and propaganda to cover up intentional exploitation of vulnerable people. Lack of testing and detrimental consequences are occurring, but organizations want the public to feel secure and safe. The very theoretical models of public health research, put in place to protect and keep one healthy, are being questioned; and when challenged by scientists and doctors themselves, are being discredited and silenced. It is concerning when individuals and society can no longer discern good from evil.

The pharaohs considered themselves gods. In Egyptian mythology, the pharaohs were the chosen ones and were viewed as direct descendants from the gods. A pharaoh was recognized by his wearing a headdress called the *uraeus* (jue'ries)—a rearing cobra. The striking cobra evoked fear, promised protection, and represented a goddess who was believed to oversee both life and death. The Egyptian serpent was a symbol of sovereignty, royalty, deity, and divine authority in ancient Egypt. The uraeus was conveyed as giving legitimacy to the ruler.

> *And the great dragon was thrown down, that ancient serpent, who is called the devil, Satan, the deceiver of the whole world—he was thrown down to the earth and his angels were thrown down with him* (Revelation 12:9).

It is interesting that the pharaohs wore serpent headdresses. To me this symbolizes the deception of the mind. It was the serpent that showed up in the Garden of Eden with subtle deception. The serpent, Satan, captivated Eve's heart—she desired fruit that she saw as good and pleasant. She perceived God was withholding something from her—rather than seeing the reality that she already had everything she needed, which includes LIFE! Of course, it didn't take her long to realize it after she was spiritually separated from the presence of God. Her sin nature would be multiplied throughout all mankind.

Today, subtle deception from the serpent has caught our eyes and captivated our hearts. We believe God is withholding from us, when in reality He has given us everything through Christ Jesus His Son, who through His death and resurrection we have been reconciled back into God's very presence and LIFE. Today, our society is bent on satisfying the desires of health, beauty, youthfulness, and fitness. Today, we want God, but only if we can be trendy and uphold cultural standards.

We want peace and tranquility—no pain, no distress, no discomfort. We desire extended length of days. Our eyes are focused on 70-80 years of life on this earth rather than life eternal. (Our eternal life began when we were created. My eternal life in the Kingdom of God began when I placed Jesus on the throne of my heart as Lord.) We will each die physically, but our soul lives on. On this earth I believe that the God who created me will sustain me. Unfortunately most eyes are fixed on the serpent symbol (medicine, public health, pharmacy, and metaphysical spiritual psychology doctrines and philosophies—to include alternative modalities that are promoted as natural and God created).

Moses and the Pharaoh

It is interesting that when Moses went to see the pharaoh, God had him throw his staff down, and it turned into a serpent. The pharaohs knew the power of magic (demons); they knew the power of the *kundalini* spirit (serpent spirit in Eastern religion, such as yoga, packaged in exercise for the West). They believed they could demonstrate power and authority. The pharaoh had magicians throw down their staffs, which also became serpents. Moses' serpent then swallowed up the other two serpents.

In Revelation, we just read about a dragon being thrown down—the same Satan will finally be disposed when Jesus comes back. However, even in Moses' time, God was demonstrating to His people that He had absolute supremacy and authority over snakes (demons)!

> *Behold, I have given you authority to tread on serpents and scorpions, all power of the enemy; nothing shall hurt you* (Luke 10:19).

Wow! Praise God!

> *But Pharaoh also called the wise men and the sorcerers; so the magicians of Egypt, they also did in like manner with their enchantments. For every man threw down his rod, and they became serpents. But Aaron's rod swallowed up their rods* (Exodus 7:11-12 NKJV).

The Bible condemns magicians, enchanters, mediums, astrologers, witches, wizards, and sorcerers. They all involve the spirit realm, specifically demonic spirits. The Hebrew word for sorcerer is *kashaph*. Sorcerers were what we would call the scientists of their day. In the modern dictionary, one would find a definition often associated with black magic or sorcery, meaning the art and practice of casting spells on people or things. Kashaph is not well defined in modern translations.

Sorcerers changed things so they took on a new appearance. In fact, tracing this word back to Middle Egyptian origins, we find it has the idea of deception through the change of imagery or appearance, such as the example given in Exodus 7 with the serpents. As we have previously seen, sorcerer in the Greek is the word *pharmakeia* where we get the word pharmacy. When people today use genetic engineering on plants and animals so that they produce substances that may be used as drugs or pharmaceuticals, it is called *pharming*. In the Bible, it is called sorcery. It is called that because its very root means to alter or change the essence of something—this is the word kashaph—to alter or change the very essence of a plant, animal, or person.

These sorcerers were in the business of using satanic or supernatural powers to alter God's creation, which was profoundly forbidden by God. Only God knows and can judge who is doing what and how, when it comes to science as it relates to sorcery. However, it is clear that altering God's creation or His Word is forbidden.

Later, we find Moses in the wilderness. The serpents were deadly. It is interesting that Moses again uses a serpent. He held up a serpent on a brass pole, and if people looked up, they were healed. People in this culture knew the significance of serpents. Yet again, God used a serpent and raised it up on a brass pole to signify the prophetic pronouncement that one day Jesus—ultimate absolute power and authority—would be raised up to die on a cross, be buried, and raised up to life again, defeating death and for our rescue, healing, and restoration—our wholeness and completeness in Him. For God so loved the world!

And as Moses lifted up the serpent in the wilderness, so must the Son of Man be lifted up, that whoever believes in him may have eternal life. For God so loved the world, that he gave his only Son, that whoever believes in him should not perish but have eternal life (John 3:14-16).

In the end, we again see in Revelation:

And the great dragon was thrown down, that ancient serpent, who is called the devil, Satan, the deceiver of the whole world—he was thrown down to the earth and his angels were thrown down with him (Revelation 12:9).

It is interesting to me that one of the ways this serpent, Satan, still deceives the whole world is captivating the desires of people, causing them to fix their eyes and place their trust in the serpent and other gods. There was a showdown of authority before Pharaoh. There was a showdown between Kingdoms at the cross of Calvary. And there will be a final showdown for all the world to witness when King Jesus returns to the earth once and for all, to reign over the entire world forever!

All Scripture is breathed out by God and profitable for teaching, for reproof, for correction, and for training in righteousness, that the man of God may be complete, equipped for every good work (2 Timothy 3:16-17).

I charge you in the presence of God and of Christ Jesus, who is to judge the living and the dead, and by his appearing and his kingdom: preach the word; be ready in season and out of season; reprove, rebuke, and exhort, with complete patience and teaching. For the time is coming when people will not endure sound teaching, but having itching ears they will accumulate for themselves teachers to suit their own passions, and will turn away from listening to the truth and wander off into myths. As for you, always be sober-minded, endure suffering, do the work of an evangelist, fulfill your ministry (2 Timothy 4:1-5).

But the Lord stood by me and strengthened me, so that through me the message might be fully proclaimed and all the Gentiles might hear it. So I was rescued from the lion's mouth. The Lord will rescue me from every evil deed and bring me safely into his heavenly kingdom. To him be the glory forever and ever. Amen (2 Timothy 4:17-18).

Don't Look Back
You are not going that way!

As Spirit-filled believers we know that God has authority and power over all kingdoms, kings, authority, and pharaohs! We are eagerly and wildly anticipating the final showdown when Jesus will return as the King and Ruler for all the world to see. We know that Jesus is the Name above all names—all names must bow to that precious, powerful Name!

Behold, I have given you authority to tread on serpents and scorpions, all power of the enemy; nothing shall hurt you (Luke 10:19).

And you were dead in the trespasses and sins in which you once walked, following the course of this world, following the prince of the power of the air, the spirit that is now at work in the sons of disobedience—among whom we all once lived in the passions of our flesh, carrying out the desires of the body and the mind, and were by nature children of wrath, like the rest of mankind. But God, being rich in mercy, because of the great love with which he loved us, even when we were dead in our trespasses, made us alive together with Christ— by grace you have been saved—and raised us up with him and seated us with him in the heavenly places in Christ Jesus, so that in the coming ages he might show the immeasurable riches of his grace in kindness toward us in Christ Jesus. For by grace you have been saved through faith. And this is not your own doing; it is the gift of God, not a result of works, so that no one may boast. For we are his workmanship, created in Christ Jesus for good works, which God prepared beforehand, that we should walk in them (Ephesians 2:1-10).

We are God's workmanship and He has given us everything for life and godliness.

His divine power has given to us all things that pertain to life and godliness, through the knowledge of Him who called us by glory and virtue, by which He has given to us exceedingly great and precious promises, so that through these you may be partakers of the divine nature, having escaped from the corruption that is in the world because of lust. For this very reason, giving all diligence, add to your faith virtue, to virtue knowledge, to knowledge self-control, to self-control perseverance, to perseverance godliness, to godliness brotherly kindness, and to brotherly kindness love. For if these things are yours and abound, you will be neither barren nor unfruitful in the knowledge of our Lord Jesus Christ. For he who lacks these things is shortsighted, even to blindness, and has forgotten that he was cleansed for his old sins (1 Peter 1:3-9 NKJV).

He himself bore our sins in his body on the tree, that we might die to sin and live to righteousness. By his wounds you have been healed (1 Peter 2:24).

Pharaoh Has Been Challenged

Ask the Holy Spirit

Why are people captivated by things that don't last, can't promise a cure, and inadvertently cause pain and torment, untoward consequences, at the risk of death or at the expense of one's soul?

Ask the Holy Spirit to examine your heart. Ask Him to show you a time in your life when you had perfect peace. Ask Him what changed. How did you respond to what changed? Did you embrace a counterfeit—a lie—that led you to pain and hopelessness? All lies lead to hopelessness!

Ask the Holy Spirit to reveal to you His truth and then embrace it not with just words but put action to your belief. When the Holy Spirit reveals truth, it will always line up with the Holy Bible—God's Word. If it does not, it is not of God and it is a lie.

Ask the Holy Spirit to give you revelation of who God is and who you are to Him. Ask Him to reveal to you what is hindering you from trusting Him. He wants to impact and be Lord in every part of you! Ask Him why you are not walking in a higher level of wellness. Are you submitting your life and trust to someone else? If we really search our hearts, you may hear things like fear or disappointment or even anger with God. What is causing your unbelief?

- Fear of death?
- Fear that God won't come through for you?
- Open doors, meaning you have given legal right for demons to create havoc in your life by participating in or viewing things of the kingdom of darkness? It is easy to be ensnared by Eastern and mystical religions (demons) that are repackaged as exercise, wellness, stress management, and metaphysical mind/body techniques.
- Anger at God because of disappointment, discouragement, or distress? Don't let Satan "dis" you by keeping you problem focused rather than promise focused!

Every word of God proves true; he is a shield to those who take refuge in him (Proverbs 30:5).

Do Not Go Down to Egypt

"Ah, stubborn children," declares the Lord, "who carry out a plan, but not mine, and who make an alliance, but not of my Spirit, that they may add sin to sin; who set out to go down to Egypt, without asking for my direction, to take refuge in the protection of Pharaoh and to seek shelter in the shadow of Egypt! Therefore shall the protection of Pharaoh turn to your shame, and the shelter in the shadow of Egypt to your humiliation. For though his officials are at Zoan and his envoys reach Hanes, everyone comes to shame through a people that cannot profit them, that brings neither help nor profit, but shame and disgrace."...Egypt's help is worthless and empty; therefore I have called her "Rahab who sits still."... For they are a rebellious people, lying children, children unwilling to hear the instruction of the Lord; who say to the seers, "Do not see," and to the prophets, "Do not prophesy to us what is right; speak to us smooth things, prophesy illusions" (Isaiah 30:1-10).

Go up to Gilead, and take balm, O virgin daughter of Egypt! In vain you have used many medicines; there is no healing for you. The nations have heard of your shame, and the earth is full of your cry; for warrior has stumbled against warrior; they have both fallen together (Jeremiah 46:11-12).

What You Don't Know Can Kill You

Where there is no prophetic vision the people cast off restraint, but blessed is he who keeps the law by mere words a servant is not disciplined for though he understands, he will not respond (Proverbs 29:18-19).

This verse is frequently misquoted—people leave off the word "prophetic," which qualifies the type of vision. The Lord clearly desires that we each hear His voice and that we know His plans, thoughts, and purposes. We frequently proclaim that vision drives everything, but what if the vision is not from God? It becomes just an idea or a self-promoted idea from a visionary person. A prophetic vision from God will be birthed in anguish—a deep internal drive because you have heard the anguish of God's heart for the lost and hurting, and those hungry for discipleship. The vision will be intentional with purpose and accompanied by supernatural provision. People will be motivated with passion and zeal because they know God's own heart and purpose.

Those that know the Word of God, read over and over the many times people forgot the power of God and His ways. They assimilated themselves with foreign cultures and their practices, to include worshipping their gods, and they soon forgot God. Over and over God looked upon their troubles and delivered them from their distress.

> *But they mixed with the nations and learned to do as they did. They served their idols, which became a snare to them. They sacrificed their sons and their daughters to the demons; they poured out innocent blood, the blood of their sons and daughters, whom they sacrificed to the idols of Canaan, and the land was polluted with blood. Thus they became unclean by their acts, and played the whore in their deeds.*
>
> *Then the anger of the Lord was kindled against his people, and he abhorred his heritage; he gave them into the hand of the nations, so that those who hated them ruled over them. Their enemies oppressed them, and they were brought into subjection under their power. Many times he delivered them, but they were rebellious in their purposes and were brought low through their iniquity. Nevertheless, he looked upon their distress, when he heard their cry. For their sake he remembered his covenant, and relented according to the abundance of his steadfast love* (Psalm 106:35-45).
>
> *Great is your mercy, O Lord; give me life according to your rules* (Psalm 119:156).

Great peace have those who love your law; nothing can make them stumble (Psalm 119:165).

If your law had not been my delight, I would have perished in my affliction (Psalm 119:92).

Fast Forward to Today

Many Christians read the Bible, but do we really know what God says in it? Do we really know the Author of the Bible—our Healer, Baptizer, and Deliverer? Life and death are at stake—not only eternal life but also life as we know it on earth.

Are you fulfilling what God has called you to do? If not, what is stopping you?

Science was intended to make inquiry and discovery revealing the glory of God and His majestic creation. The tide has turned—science is reported to have become a corrupted network of multiple collaborating institutional stakeholders and policy makers doing great harm to human beings.

Dr. Judy Mikovits (2017), the former Director of the Lab of Anti-Viral Drug Mechanisms at the National Cancer Research Institute, has come forward, along with other colleagues from medicine and science, for the sole purpose of making the public aware of such practices. She is a scientist with more than 50 published research studies in immunology and virology. She herself was the leading researcher in the study that discovered retroviruses from animal tissue in vaccines are responsible for the explosion of devastating chronic diseases such as autoimmune diseases, Chronic Fatigue Syndrome, Fibromyalgia, neurological problems, brain disorders, autism, and cancers.

Forever, O Lord, your word is firmly fixed in the heaven (Psalm 119:89).

The word "forever" is the Hebrew pictograph *lamed* of a shepherd's staff used to direct sheep by pushing or pulling them. It was

Pharaoh Has Been Challenged

also used as a weapon against predators to defend and protect the sheep. The meaning of this letter is "toward" as moving something in a different direction. This letter also means "authority," as it is a sign of the shepherd, the leader of the flock. It also means "yoke," which is a staff on the shoulders, "tie" or "bind" from idea of the yoke that is bound to the animal. (http://www.ancient-hebrew.org/alphabet_letters_lamed.html)

Forever, O Lord, Your word is settled in heaven. Your faithfulness endures to all generations. You have established the earth and it abides (Psalm 119:89-90 NKJV).

This text asserts the all-encompassing, absolute, and authoritative Word over our lives. The Word of God is unchangingly secured in heaven and nothing or no one can change it. 1) Though seasons change, cultures and worldviews change, or governments and philosophies change, they have no effect on God's Word and His authority. 2) God is faithful at applying His power, promise, and blessing of His Word, along with justice and judgement in His spoken word for living. 3) While all creation responds to God's Word, man is often in contrast in his submission to his Creator God's Words.

As spiritual people we are to refuse the natural inclinations of fallen men. As we hear and yield to the authority of God's Word, we are privileged to walk in His divine refuge, protection, and healing. What is being exposed in science, medicine, and psychology should be a wakeup call to the church to repent, turn back to God, and stand upon His Word for salvation (*sozo*-wholeness, restoration, deliverance, healing, rescue, provision).

How awesome it is that the Hebrew picture word for this passage gives us a glimpse of Jesus! His yoke is easy and His burden is light. Thank God that our Father always does what He says He will do—His Word is fixed! Jesus is our Peace—nothing missing, nothing broken, nothing lacking.

If your law had not been my delight, I would have perished in my affliction (Psalm 119:92).

I am severely afflicted; give me life, O Lord, according to your word! (Psalm 119:107)

Great peace have those who love your law; nothing can make them stumble (Psalm 119:165).

Keep steady my step according to your promise and let no iniquity get dominion over me (Psalm 119:33).

I am so thankful for professionals like Dr. Judy Mikovits and the others coming forth to expose the man-made epidemics and new devastating diseases and deaths affecting more than one generation of people. She and others are attempting to get our government to place a hold on all immunizations and have independent researchers be the quality monitor individuals instead of the agencies self-reporting the data. For more information about the reports of fraud crimes and misconceptions behind the world's vaccine and pharmaceutical companies, described by Dr. Mikovits, the book, *Plague* (2014/2017) is an excellent resource.

The book is about her journey through 35 years of science in pursuit of truth. Vaccines and autism are two highly charged political topics around the world. She currently uses her platforms for public awareness and education. The following paragraphs are an attempt to briefly summarize key thoughts from the book.

Dr. Mikovitz brings a shocking message of what happens when government agencies, pharmaceutical companies, and health care systems sponsor science and go unchecked and unchallenged. She reports that the medical community does not want to look at the question why mouse retroviruses have jumped into the human population.

Dr. Mikovitz reports various studies, to include one colleague that discovered the link between MMR—Measles, Mumps, Rubella—vaccine and autism. She reports that as a scientist, she can give a solid, real-science answer to why parents observed a change in their children after they receive a vaccine—that yes, they were normal before the vaccine and afterwards they were not. She reported crimes against humanity and breach of ethics research in various health agencies that have been going on for many decades. Doctors are forced to trust what is recommended by these agencies, for example, the U.S. frequent vaccine schedule.

Dr. Judy's sole purpose as a scientist was to investigate why people are sick so that we could find solutions for improvement. Instead, she found that the vaccine toxins, animal retroviruses, and the metals (mercury and aluminum) are making people chronically ill, develop autism and neurological damage, contract cancer, and experience early death. She also discovered that 4-8% of the healthy human population is carrying the mouse retrovirus.

She further described that in 1994, the scientific community reported concerns and the real possibility that growing human virus in animal tissues and cells around the world, and injecting them back into humans could introduce animal viruses into the human population. The research conducted by Dr. Mikovits in 2011 shows that this catastrophe had already happened.

She and many colleagues are calling for freedom advocacy groups in every state to educate the public and to take back your rights to make your own decisions for you and your family. She reports that to this day, millions of people stay desperately ill with no cure. The very immune activation that was supposed to confer immunity for one virus ends up causing newly discovered retroviruses that harm humans. Dr. Mikovits estimates conservatively that one in fifty children are now affected with autism related to the transplant of animal virus into humans. In autism spectrum disorders and the chronic illnesses induced by this retrovirus, people do not recover. She credits her faith in God that has propelled her through her ordeal. She stated that God never intended for animal viruses to be injected into the human bloodstream.

It is our responsibility to pray for these individuals and pray that God would supernaturally turn around evil that causes harm. God has not changed. His Son, Jesus, made it possible that those who trust and obey are healed and delivered. He has given us authority over the demonic realm operating to harm us.

Xenotransplantation
This refers to the growing of tissue or cells in an animal and then transplanting it back into a human. Xenotransplantation can be organs, tissues, or cells. *Xeno* is the Greek word meaning "foreign." According to Dr. Mikovits, in 1995, there were discussions in the scientific community about the dangers of xenograft approaches commonly used in the study of human cancer, which is known to promote the development of novel retroviruses with pathogenic properties.

Autism Denial
Another stunning discovery was found and published as a book called, *Denial: How Refusing to Face the Facts about Our Autism Epidemic Hurts Children and Families* (2017) by Olsted, D. and Bloxill, M. These authors herald a call for scientific research to be heard and a call for action by the public health community and pharmaceutical companies to stop vaccines because they are not safe. These researchers report timelines and history of autism and subsequent causative factors, which are vaccines. They report that autism was in effect zero percent before 1930, and in the 1980s it began to rise sharply. Now they conclude the same as others in research that 1 in 50 children have developed autism spectrum syndrome.

Again, it seems as we assimilate philosophies of the world in trusting the expertise of man, rather than the expertise of our Creator, we don't consider the consequences. God so clearly called us out to be a separate and distinct people. What makes us distinct? We know the Creator, Father God, personally! He is still our

Healer and nothing, absolutely nothing is impossible with God. Set your eyes and heart on Him—watch Him do the impossible! Praise You, God, You are too marvelous for words!

It is now our responsibility to pray for these individuals and that God will supernaturally turn around the evil that causes harm. God has not changed, His Son Jesus made it possible that those who trust and obey God are healed and delivered and have authority over the demonic realm operating to harm.

Oh God, We *Really* Need You!

I will lift up my eyes to the hills—from whence comes my help? My help comes from the Lord, Who made heaven and earth. He will not allow your foot to be moved; He who keeps you will not slumber (Psalm 121:1-3 NKJV).

The Lord shall preserve you from all evil; He shall preserve your soul . The Lord shall preserve your going out and your coming in from this time forth, and even forevermore (Psalm 121:7-8 NKJV).

There should be a public outcry for why we are genetically manipulating or altering the genes of future generations in unknown ways that are incapacitating and deadly. Why is there not one? It is easy to see why truth is suppressed and hidden when conflicts of interest arise within a convoluted network of sponsors of research funding, regulatory agencies, and politics, each developing their own credibility and identity as portrayed to the public. When God is not a factor in the works of man, it is natural for men to define what is ethical and acceptable to meet their own needs and definition of truth. The bottom line, however, is that the network of these national and world agencies promote health policy that influence, and sometimes mandate, such things as standards of practice for treatments and drug therapy related to physical disease and mental health, as well as types of vaccine schedules. This should concern Christian believers greatly and compel people to get on their knees before God, repent, fast, and pray for the healing of our nation.

I see these type findings and information related to such a huge network as a betrayal of public trust, which should be a wakeup call for all those that proclaim God as their source of life! This scenario reminds me again of Pharaoh controlling and oppressing God's people. Today, people are placing their trust in systems and products instead of God, only to find themselves enslaved and trapped in chemical restraints and a downward spiral of chronic illness and death. The Pharaonic anti-Christ spirits in the U.S. are operating—promising protection, yet evoking fear—and declaring to the world that they are the authority over life and death, as our body and health freedoms are being taken. However, this Pharaonic spirit over this territory has now been challenged in the name of Jesus!

Be wise, let the Lord counsel you through His Word. Let's be careful, it is not the intent to condemn or accuse or slander anyone. An anti-Christ spirit is operating through these entities and people who do evil. However, God's mercy and steadfast love are everlasting. Pray for Dr. Judy Mikovits and her colleagues coming forth in truth—pray for open doors and avenues of communication for them to make legislative changes. Pray for all the scientists and stakeholders that they would discover God's glory and majestic hand in creation and turn towards Him. He can change hearts! God will bring good from what Satan meant for harm. Even more compelling, pray that those that profess to be God's people will return to Him and will have greater revelation of who He is and His amazing love for us—that people will return to trust Him for everything, especially life!

> *My son, be attentive to my words; incline your ear to my sayings. Let them not escape from your sight; keep them within your heart. For they are life to those who find them, and healing to all their flesh. Keep your heart with all vigilance, for from it flow the springs of life. Put away from you crooked speech, and put devious talk far from you.*

Let your eyes look directly forward, and your gaze be straight before you (Proverbs 4:20-25).

Your testimonies are my delight; they are my counselors (Psalm 119:24).

Your testimonies are wonderful; therefore, my soul keeps them (Psalm 119:129).

It is time for You to act, Oh Lord, for they have regarded Your law as void (Psalm 119:126).

The Perfect Storm

- Man-made epidemics and chronic illnesses and cancers, tormenting deaths
- Man-made genetic mutations
- No cures
- Suppression of truth from those in authority and medical experts
- Freedom of health choices restricted
- Psychology false doctrines and philosophies, non-scientific labeling and diagnoses
- Pharmaceutical industry producing deadly drugs and governing agencies making policy and mandates exploiting those that do not have the equivalent field knowledge as control for trust and compliance

God is calling His body of Christ followers out of Egypt! We have already been delivered but are not walking in the fullness of God's power—dead-raising, miracle working power—as He told us we could. We have not been separated as a distinct and resolute people, making disciples with God and confirming His Word. He's setting us up for an opportunity to minister healing and deliverance to gather a harvest of souls that have been crying out for help.

We must seek Him! Repent, turn from your unbelief and ways of the world, and set your eyes and heart on Jesus!

Jesus slept through storms! He comes from a place where there are no storms. Jesus calmed the storms! He gave what He already had in Him—Peace. Divine Healing—Shalom Peace—JESUS—the answer to it all! God is still our Healer—even autism and brain disorders and chronic disease.

The Great Commission

And he said to them, "Go into all the world and proclaim the gospel to the whole creation. Whoever believes and is baptized will be saved, but whoever does not believe will be condemned. And these signs will accompany those who believe: in my name they will cast out demons; they will speak in new tongues; they will pick up serpents with their hands; and if they drink any deadly poison, it will not hurt them; they will lay their hands on the sick, and they will recover."

So then the Lord Jesus, after he had spoken to them, was taken up into heaven and sat down at the right hand of God. And they went out and preached everywhere, while the Lord worked with them and confirmed the message by accompanying signs (Mark 16:15-20 NKJV).

Behold, I give you the authority to trample on serpents and scorpions, and over all the power of the enemy, and nothing shall by any means hurt you (Luke 10:19 NKJV).

What Do We Do?

We repent, turn from sin and unbelief, and return to God. Examine your heart—what is the last thing God told you to do—are you doing it? Examine your spiritual foundation—have you been baptized in water? Baptized in the Holy Spirit? If so, then the Bible tells us to put on the full armor of God so that we may be able to stand against the devil—to stand firm, praying continually in the Spirit (Ephesians 6). Matthew 6:33 tells us to seek first the

Kingdom of God and His righteousness. Philippians tells us not to be anxious for anything but rejoice with thanksgiving, make our requests before God, and He will provide all of our needs. We can trust God to take care of those who are His!

We also know that this is an awesome age of opportunity to share God's grace and plan of redemption with others. People are desperate for hope; we can introduce them to Jesus so that each can find Life!

> *Finally, be strong in the Lord and in the strength of his might. Put on the whole armor of God, that you may be able to stand against the schemes of the devil. For we do not wrestle against flesh and blood, but against the rulers, against the authorities, against the cosmic powers over this present darkness, against the spiritual forces of evil in the heavenly places. Therefore take up the whole armor of God, that you may be able to withstand in the evil day, and having done all, to stand firm. Stand therefore, having fastened on the belt of truth, and having put on the breastplate of righteousness, and, as shoes for your feet, having put on the readiness given by the gospel of peace. In all circumstances take up the shield of faith, with which you can extinguish all the flaming darts of the evil one; and take the helmet of salvation, and the sword of the Spirit, which is the word of God, praying at all times in the Spirit, with all prayer and supplication. To that end, keep alert with all perseverance, making supplication for all the saints* (Ephesians 6:10-18).

> *But seek first the kingdom of God and his righteousness, and all these things will be added to you* (Matthew 6:33).

> *Rejoice in the Lord always; again I will say, rejoice. Let your reasonableness be known to everyone. The Lord is at hand; do not be anxious about anything, but in everything by prayer and supplication with thanksgiving let your requests be made known to God. And the peace of God, which surpasses all understanding, will guard your hearts and your minds in Christ Jesus. Finally, brothers, whatever is true, whatever is honorable, whatever is just, whatever is pure,*

whatever is lovely, whatever is commendable, if there is any excellence, if there is anything worthy of praise, think about these things. What you have learned and received and heard and seen in me—practice these things, and the God of peace will be with you.

And my God will supply every need of yours according to his riches in glory in Christ Jesus. To our God and Father be glory forever and ever. Amen (Philippians 4:4-9; 19-20).

TESTIMONY

Praise God, He is teaching me to totally depend on Him. I stopped taking medicines many years ago. I underwent an unexpected hysterectomy when I was 33 years of age. I was told that I would be on hormone replacement for the greater part of the rest of my life. I am thankful that when I moved to another state a few years later, my doctor told me that I needed to get off the estrogen because there are problems with its long-term use.

However, he prescribed a drug called Actonel, which was a pill taken weekly. He told me that I didn't have osteopenia yet (a precursor to osteoporosis—loss of calcium in the bone which makes them brittle); however, I fit the classical description for high risk to develop it: tall, small bone frame, and fair-skinned. So I got the prescription and began taking the drug. After the second week, I did not feel settled in my spirit about taking it because of the potential side effects: bone and joint pain, headaches, eye pain and /or itching, esophageal irritation, and bladder cancer. Today the same drug is reported to have these same effects as well as others such as fractures, osteonecrosis (bone death), esophageal cancer, and can cause severe allergic reactions, which include severe burning and peeling of the skin!

I stopped taking it after two doses and threw the prescription away. Today, getting closer to retirement age, I am healthy and have great bones. I am able to exercise, hike, and have never had broken bones. I chose that day to believe God is who He says He is, and that He always does what He says—that is a good, good Father!

Since then, I have stopped taking vaccinations, even the annual flu shot; I haven't taken Tylenol or any analgesics in 15 years. I choose to believe God. Sometimes I get a headache or sore muscles from a work out, but I work through it, thanking Jesus for my healing because of what He did for me on the Cross until it goes away. It always goes away—sometimes quickly and sometimes it takes longer. A few years ago, I came down with flu-like symptoms, and many people had it. I took the day off, made hot soup, rested, and kept hydrated! I let my own immune system handle it. Yes, it is normal to have a fever—that lets you know the immune system is working. I was over my symptoms in less than 24 hours while most people took days. My cough lasted 2-3 days while those around me took weeks; they were all medicated supposedly to help them!

I am not telling people what to do. I am telling people to develop an intimate relationship with Jesus! Watch Him work as you let Him reveal Himself to you through His Word and through the Holy Spirit, not just for healing, but every aspect of your life. In John 6:63-6, Jesus said, "The words that I have spoken to you are spirit and life. But there are some of you who do not believe."

My final authority is always the Bible. I thank God for experiences that have helped me grasp the revelation of God's Word and He means what He says. I am thankful that He fashions, directs, and establishes our footsteps if we surrender to Him to do it. Get into His Word—seek God the Healer and not the healing. The Holy Spirit will illuminate what you see and do through God's Word. Whatever He says, just do it.

Be not wise in your own eyes; fear the Lord, and turn away from evil. It will be healing to your flesh and refreshment to your bones (Proverbs 3:7-8).

He keeps all his bones, not one of them is broken (Psalm 34:20).

A joyful heart is good medicine, but a broken spirit dries up the bones (Proverbs 17:22).

My son, be attentive to my words; incline your ear to my sayings. Let them not escape from your sight; keep them within your heart. For they are life to those who find them, and healing to all their flesh. Keep your heart with all vigilance, for from it flow the springs of life. Put away from you crooked speech, and put devious talk far from you. Let your eyes look directly forward, and your gaze be straight before you (Proverbs 4:20-25).

Get in God's Word, focus on God's Word, believe and act on God's Word!

Renew your mind by the Word of God, and you will know the good, acceptable, and perfect will of God. God loves you and He has given us everything for life and godliness. He wants you well!

I beseech you therefore, brethren, by the mercies of God, that you present your bodies a living sacrifice, holy, acceptable to God, which is your reasonable service. And do not be conformed to this world, but be transformed by the renewing of your mind, that you may prove what is that good and acceptable and perfect will of God (Romans 12:1-2 NKJV).

Are You Desperate Yet?

God has always had a plan for reconciliation. There is no Plan B; the Holy Spirit has no substitutes!

Back to the Beginning—Genesis 1:1-28

"In the beginning God created the heavens and the earth" (Genesis 1:1). In verse 11, God created vegetation, plants, and trees yielding seed according to their own kind—and God saw it was good. He goes on to create the great sea creatures and every living water creature that moves, according to their own kinds, and every winged bird according to its kind. And God said it was good. Next, God created more living creatures according to its kinds—livestock according to their kinds and creeping things according to their own kinds, and beasts of the earth according to their own kinds. The common denominator for plants and animals is that each was created after their own kinds.

Later, in verse 26, God said,

Let us make man in our own image after our likeness. And let them have dominion over the fish and over the birds of the heavens and over livestock and over all the earth and over every creeping thing that creeps on the earth.

Wait, what? Man in God's own image! Each species was created into existence each according to their kinds. Man is totally separated from plants and animals; he was made in God's own image—that is pretty amazing! God from the beginning made man distinct and separate from everything else.

Some Christians have used Genesis 1:26 to mean that man has the ability to create and recreate like God. This thought pattern is used to justify practices when there are ethical arguments concerning animals. Others have used the word "dominion" as permission to experiment and make improvements to better mankind. It was never God's intent to mix animal and human tissue or to place animal tissue into human blood. I can't even imagine God being pleased, especially since He hears the cries of those suffering in torment, with disabilities and death due to the consequences. The Bible says that the blood is the life of an animal.

> *For the life of every creature is its blood: its blood is life, therefore, I have said to the people of Israel, you should not eat blood of any creature for the life of every creature is its blood. Whoever eats will be cut off* (Leviticus 17:14).

Thank God for His grace and protection and my source of life. We can now live under God's protection, His authority, and His supernatural intervention. Not only sin, but disease has been defeated at the Cross of Calvary by Jesus Himself! Jesus' blood was shed to give us life. What good news! That is grace—I did not deserve it!

The blood of Jesus is more powerful than you can ever imagine! The blood of Jesus has the power to release the grip of any curse or bondage that has afflicted man.

> *He himself bore our sins in his body on the tree, that we might die to sin and live to righteousness. By his wounds you have been healed* (1 Peter 2:24).

> *And after you have suffered a little while, the God of all grace, who has called you to his eternal glory in Christ, will restore, confirm, strengthen, and establish you. To Him be dominion forever and ever. Amen* (1 Peter 5:10-11).

> *His divine power has granted to us all things that pertain to life and godliness, through the knowledge of him who called us to his own glory and excellence, by which he has granted to us his precious and very great promises, so that through them you may become partakers of the divine nature, having escaped from the corruption that is in the world because of sinful desire* (2 Peter 1:3-5).

God's Promise—Himself

Before Jesus ascended into heaven, He instructed His disciples to wait for the promise of the Father. In Acts 2, we see the Pentecostal experience when the sound as like a mighty rushing wind came into the upper room—tongues of fire rested on each person's head, and they began speaking other languages. The disciples whom Jesus had rebuked for their unbelief earlier, walked out of their weakness into a "dead-raising" power to do what God called them to do.

Absolutely the best teaching resource that I have encountered on the subject of the Holy Spirit, besides the Holy Spirit Himself, is found in *Holy Spirit: Are You Flammable or Fireproof?* by Evangelist Reinhard Bonnke. Reinhard Bonnke is the founder of Christ for All Nations, a ministry known for conducting great Gospel crusades throughout the continent of Africa and around the world. He preaches the full Gospel under the strong anointing of the Holy Spirit for salvation and healing. Yes, Rev. Bonnke has witnessed many miracles, including witnessing many times the dead raised to life!

Peter began teaching that this experience was the Holy Spirit—the fulfillment of the prophecy given by the Old Testament prophet, Joel. The people around Peter asked him, "Brothers, what shall we do?"

Peter said to them, "Repent and be baptized every one of you in the name of Jesus Christ for the forgiveness of your sins, and you will receive the gift of the Holy Spirit. For the promise is for you and for your children and for all who are far off—everyone whom the Lord calls to Himself" (Acts 2:38-39).

God Is Wooing People Back to Himself— We choose!

We always choose! Who can receive this precious and priceless gift? Everyone who makes Jesus Lord!

The Holy Spirit is the third Person of the Trinity—He is God Himself impacting all of us! The Holy Spirit is a Person, not an "it." The "it" is the evidence of speaking in a new language. The experience is not just a one-time event—He is a continual power flow expressed in us and through us. Reinhard Bonnke describes the language as mortal man having conversation in perfect communion with his Father in heaven.

Speaking in tongues is the sign of the potential. The Holy Spirit wants to permeate your whole being; however, the Kingdom of God is ruled by a King. This means it is not a democracy, a senate committee, and there are no majority votes. Jesus is perfect theology and absolute authority. Nothing—no institutions, diseases, labels, drugs—have power over the Kingdom of God. What God says or decrees is final. It is spiritual law! What we do, then, is proclaim what has been already decreed by God. The enemy knows he and his cohorts are under the authority of Jesus, but he also knows whether or not you believe he is. God's plan is unfolding before our eyes—the time is so short. God's Word says it all!

> *Behold, I have given you authority to tread on serpents and scorpions, and over all the power of the enemy, and nothing shall hurt you* (Luke 10:19).

> *And he said to them, "Go into all the world and proclaim the gospel to the whole creation. Whoever believes and is baptized will be saved, but whoever does not believe will be condemned. And these signs will accompany those who believe: in my name they will cast out demons; they will speak in new tongues; they will pick up serpents with their hands; and if they drink any deadly poison, it will not hurt them; they will lay their hands on the sick, and they will recover."*

> *So then the Lord Jesus, after he had spoken to them, was taken up into heaven and sat down at the right hand of God. And they went out and preached everywhere, while the Lord worked with them and confirmed the message by accompanying signs* (Mark 16:15-20).

> *Now the eleven disciples went to Galilee, to the mountain to which Jesus had directed them. And when they saw him they worshiped him, but some doubted. And Jesus came and said to them, "All authority in heaven and on earth has been given to me. Go therefore and make*

disciples of all nations, baptizing them in the name of the Father and of the Son and of the Holy Spirit, teaching them to observe all that I have commanded you. And behold, I am with you always, to the end of the age" (Matthew 28:16-20).

What professing Christians don't understand is that the power is the essence of the Christian witness—it is supernatural or absolutely nothing at all! —*Reinhard Bonnke*

Everything about Christianity is supernatural: the Bible, God's Word, the Cross of Calvary, and the Holy Spirit living. The creation was supernatural; Jesus and the entire Gospel is supernatural. So when we take miracles and the baptism of the Holy Spirit out of Christianity, we have taken the life out of Christianity altogether, and it becomes an empty religion. In Ephesians 1:18-20, Paul prays for "the eyes of your heart may be enlighten in order that you might know … His incomparable power for us who believe." It is in Him that "we live, and move, have our being" (Acts 17:28).

Summarizing a few of Reinhard Bonnke's (2017) "Fire Points," The Holy Spirit is:

1. **The God of Wonders** –
   - The Gospel is always fresh—just like electricity—the encounter is ageless.
   - Through baptism of the Holy Spirit, we have access to a dead-raising resurrection power.
   - He is unstoppable unless we limit Him.
   - God causes all things to work together for good of those who love God.
   - The Holy Spirit was not given on a condition that we are perfect. He was given because we are actually not perfect. He came because we really need Him. (Holy Spirit, I really need You!)

God is not just supernatural, He is miraculous by nature and so is His Spirit. To have the Spirit is to expect the miraculous, to believe the Spirit is to believe in the miraculous, and to walk in the Spirit is to move and work in the miraculous. You were made for signs and wonders! —*Reinhard Bonnke*

Baptism means to be totally immersed—your entire being—spirit, soul, body—into the Holy Spirit. This is the same Spirit that was on the Old Testament prophets. This same Spirit is in us so we should expect the same results and outcomes. PTL!

2. **The Love of Jesus!** The love of Jesus and the Holy Spirit are inseparable.

Receive Him to be your present help. Surrender to God and let Him take His place as the Lord of your life—as Savior, Healer, and Deliverer. The Holy Spirit will be the best Counselor and Comforter because He is wisdom, understanding, and might. He will help you discern wise choices and give you courage to stand firm in His Word.

Being baptized in the Holy Spirit means real enablement, strength in character, healing in our body, and divine protection. It means favor and the goodness of God we need to live life. We are living Psalm 78:40-43—how often they provoked Him in the wilderness because they did not remember His power and the works of His signs and wonders. God is calling us to Him—those that have ears to hear, let them hear.

3. **A Mighty Wind and Fire Combination.**
    - The apostles were not praying for the Spirit, but He came to invade the place!
    - Because of Jesus the heavens are open—the baptism in the Spirit is a bridge from heaven to earth.
    - Satan and his demons have no power to deprive God's citizens in His Kingdom.

We are brought into the same reality as we will know in heaven. Man, so let's walk in that reality!

Let us then with confidence draw near to the throne of grace, that we may receive mercy and find grace to help in time of need (Hebrews 4:16).

4. **People Aflame!**
   - We have the Holy Spirit in person and power.
   - You don't need more anointing or more of God—you have all of Him and His fullness.

If you are washed in the blood of Jesus, no one or nothing can separate you from Him or pluck you out of His hand. Surrender to Him, believe that He is truly there, and begin to see the manifestations of His Presence in your life. We really can be 'anxious for nothing and with everything give thanks'!

For you have died, and your life is hidden with Christ in God (Colossians 3:3).

Testimony

Several years ago, my son injured his knee shortly after high school graduation. In the Fall, he was planning to attend Master's Commission (MC), a leadership discipleship program designed for young adults transitioning to college and career tracks. His injury resulted in a loose ligament and a hole in his knee cap. The surgeon gave three options, all involving surgery repair that included a possible bone graft and a rehab period that would most likely prevent him from attending MC until the next year.

Internally, I was outraged at the enemy! I knew that this was the enemy attempting to steal or delay my son's purpose and destiny to what God had called him. I sat my family down in the living room and began to tell them that we were not going to accept this report. I prayed over my son and declared what Jesus had done—"It is written, by His stripes, my son is already healed."

Over the next few days, my son was instructed to prevent further injury by not putting weight on his leg, therefore he had to use crutches. I saw him put weight on it, and I started to get upset and say something to him. Before I could give voice to my thoughts, the Holy Spirit said, "If he is healed, why should you care if he puts weight on it?" So I kept my mouth shut and gave the Lord praise.

My husband and I arrived for surgery with my son. Upon entering the reception area, I was fighting disappointment, but kept saying, "No, this is just not reality, in Jesus' name." We watched my son be taken off to surgery and were escorted to the waiting area. What seemed just a few minutes later, the surgeon came out to talk with us. He was nervous and highly stressed. He said to us two different times, "I promise you, there really was a hole, but it's not there!" He went on to say that the loose ligament that caused the knee cap to dislocate was tightly in place. In fact, he said he tried to pry it loose and couldn't because it was like brand new. He said he just cleaned out the knee area while he was in there and then closed it. He kept saying that we were "really, really lucky!" We said, "No, it was really, really God!"

Needless to say, my son went on to fulfill what God had for him to attend on time. The pain attempted to return, but he took authority over it, the pain left, and he has not needed surgery at all. In fact, when it happened, he called me, and said, "Mom, this Kingdom stuff really works!" Yes, my child, the Kingdom of God is real because our Dad, the King, decrees His Word so!

TESTIMONY

After college graduation, my daughter was called to do an extended mission assignment. This consisted of groups of young adults traveling to multiple countries and several continents for several months with a backpack! In prepping for the trip she asked me about taking anti-malaria medications. They perceived that if God called them to go, then He would protect them. My first feeling was fear, but I could not give voice to that because somehow I knew she was right.

As a nurse, I already knew that the medications were not without potential side effects, and depending on which one, some very serious. I consulted one of the campus physicians. He said that it was not good to take for that length of time. He said it was important to give the liver a rest every couple of months. That totally did not make sense to me because my question was, "Do the mosquitos take a month off periodically?" What do missionaries do? I told my daughter that I supported her decision.

At the end of the adventure and multiple mosquito bites later, her team members who simply trusted God never contracted malaria to this day. Interestingly, the team members that did take medications contracted malaria, one being severe enough to be sent home prior to completion of the mission.

God does take care of those who love and trust Him. This generation needs to know the God of the Bible really loves them, is powerful, and honors His Word.

Don't you just want to worship God? In your prayer time, worship Him by telling Him, "God, You truly are the Way and the Truth. You really do keep your promises—You truly do miracles. Thank You, Jesus, You truly are the answer to it all!"

So What About Those Oils?

Complementary or Alternative medicine is also a huge industry—created because people are seeking alternatives to traditional models of modern medical care and searching for natural remedies and nutrition.

We have already discussed the consequences of genetically altered animals and human cells—it is no different in plants. However, God will sort all that out! I can't control what is being placed in our food, but my prayers take on new meaning when I pray before I eat.

The concerns I do raise are to make Christians aware that alternative health therapies are not always what they seem to be on the surface. Again, Satan is the ultimate counterfeit; his deception is subtle. It wouldn't be called deception, if people could see demons. When disguised as an angel of light, many Christians are blindly attracted to him out of their own desires—not God's Word. Beware, it is not always the products or the exercises but how they are packaged and delivered that is troublesome.

From a health care educator perspective, concerns about using essential oils is the same perspective as taking precautions with any prescription or over-the-counter (OTC) drug.

1. **The frequency and amounts being ingested or absorbed into the body.**

    - Oils are concentrated—regardless of what is marketed, there are no accuracy for doses.

    - Plants have always been a base for medicines, as well as those produced synthetically. Natural plant medicine is not new. Heroin, morphine, and codeine come from the poppy; aspirin is from willow bark.

    - If one is using oils to substitute for pharmaceuticals and supplements, why are people taking them when one is asymptomatic (no symptoms) or healthy?

2. **People are being told they are safe and have no side effects.**
   It is not true—there is no evidence that they are safe and without side effects. Aloe vera, for example, is a lotion most people use for burns, wound healing, or analgesic—no problem. Long-term effects, though, are heart irregularities (dysrhythmias), edema, neuropathies and hematuria or blood in the urine (Popoola, 2015). Even when diluted—there is a variation in the dosages. Lavender and tea leaf, for example, caused endocrine disruptions, which have effects similar to estrogen and have been linked to breast growth in young boys (gynecomastia) before they reached puberty as published in the *New England Journal of Medicine* (Henley, Lipson, and Korach 2007). On the other hand, tea leaf ointment has been shown to be an agent against staphylococcus aureus (staph infections), which is great. However, just like other drugs, when people overuse them, strains may become resistant. The golden standard of practice to prevent staph infections is still good handwashing!

- Giving children unnecessary "drugs"—oils without information regarding dosage and known physiological processes, is concerning. Drugs affect the liver and kidneys. They are promoted as a boost to the immune system. Foreign substances cause inflammatory responses. The underlying problem with many of the chronic and autoimmune diseases in adults involve suppression or a chronic state of inflammatory responses that cause disabilities and illness.

- False promotion of chemical free. Yes, they are chemical compounds with real chemical properties and names. There are allergic reactions and have warnings not to drink or ingest.

The point here is that each one of us should take responsibility for our physical health just like we are expected to do for our spiritual health. Research and know what you are taking and why you are taking it. More importantly, know your source of truth! Just because a company, product, or exercise regimen promotes themselves as Christian means nothing.

From a spiritual perspective and disciple-making mandate from Jesus, the concern I have with essential oils is that they are packaged in promotion as to be harmless to Christians.

1. **The promotion of oils as teaching the healing in the Bible is misleading and relating the oils to the ministry of Jesus—is absolutely false.**
   - Yes, plants were used in Egyptian and other ancient cultures. The anointing of oil used by the disciples did not heal when people prayed for the sick—Jesus healed because of who He is. It is through His death, burial, and resurrection for the remission of our sins and to reconcile us back to God—the finished work on Calvary—the atonement is why we receive healing. We lay hands on the sick as disciples, but it is Jesus in us working through us. Not oils or the laying on of the hands. Salvation, healing, deliverance (*sozo-* wholeness) is a gift from God, His Grace that we receive by our faith in Him and not faith in oils. The oil as referred to in James 5:14-15 is symbolic of the Holy Spirit; it does not contain a life force or healing properties.
   - Some companies are promoting "Come learn the art of healing like Jesus healed." Again, Jesus alone went to the Cross—His death was not an art. Being a disciple of Jesus is not an art—it is a relationship with a Person. We don't seek healing; we seek the Healer! Exercises or techniques using oil and energy are from Eastern mystic religions with philosophies that require channeling of energy—blending with the teachings of Jesus is an anti-Christ spirituality.
   - The oils are promoted as used in the Bible to anoint and heal. The actual teaching from essential oil companies is a spiritual alternative medicine modality called "energy

healing"and is described below. David Steward (2012—*Healing Oils of the Bible*) begins with the introduction:

> "The healing oils of the Bible are all essential or aromatic. These oils are the vital fluids of plants that are their life blood. They are called 'essential' because they are necessary for the life of the plant and contain the 'essence' of the plant. Essential oils contain life force, intelligence, and vibrational energy that imbues them with healing power that works for people" (Introduction, page xv). He goes on to say, "they used aromatic oils for every purpose from maintaining wellness, to physical healing, to enhancement of spiritual states in worship, to emotional cleansing, to purification from sin" (page xvi). Lastly, still in the introduction, Dr. Steward states: "Word is vibration, a frequency, a consciousness, an expression of energy. When God created the plants by his speaking voice, he imbued them with his Word and his intelligence. This includes the oils of the plants which he intended, from their very creation, to become our medicines when we need healing. That is what is so special about essential oils. They contain power from God's Word. Artificial medicines, made by humans, contain no such power. That is why they cannot heal and never will."…" The point here is that essential oils are divinely ordained as medicines for God's children and are meant to be used with God's guidance, accompanied with prayer"(page xvii).

- *Energy healing* modalities will talk about a "life force." This life force interpretation and subsequent spiritual experience people encounter is not the Holy Spirit. A counterfeit Holy Spirit is being embraced.

- Scripture is misappropriated and misinterpreted causing people to embrace this spirituality as Christianity. People are vulnerable to demonic spirits invading their life because they are actually embracing another gospel—not the Jesus of the Bible. Detail on specific biblical contradictions cited in the book, *Anointing Oils of the Bible* by Dr. David Steward, can be found in a Position Paper at Zoe Healing Center - www.zoehealingcenter.com.

2. **Some companies promote the oils as anointing oils but are taught as life force energy. People are opening themselves up to and activating the spirit realm of the occult. This creates havoc in their lives as well as negatively influencing their belief in God.**

Take heed that no one deceives you. For many will come in My name saying, 'I am the Christ', and will deceive many (Matthew 24:4-5).

For the time will come when they will not endure sound doctrine, but according to their own desires, because they have itching ears, they will heap up for themselves teachers; and they will turn away from the truth and be turned aside to fables (2 Timothy 4:3-4).

A sign of the end of the ages: massive deception! Do not be deceived. These scriptures imply that we have the ability to avoid deception and we can choose not to be deceived. Fables replace truth.

The point is that the time has come when teachers and leaders will use the same words in the Bible, even Scriptures to create fables, twisting the Word of God, which is deception. People would rather hear fables than the truth. Don't just read or listen to the words used, find out about their meaning. What do people mean when they use terms like God, life, healing, prosperity, spirit, nature, universe, empowerment, energy, spiritual awareness, personal growth, inner strength, balance, or true self?

Spirituality Connection? In Oils?

The information below includes actual essential oil names and

Pharaoh Has Been Challenged

their purposes as cited in a particular brochure and website. Holistic health includes body, mind, and spirit. Ironically, the expensive oils I reviewed had warnings to avoid direct sunlight after application, and bottles must be stored in a dark place. Oh, and did I mention, oils are expensive? Grace is a gift with unlimited anointing!

> **Forgiveness Essential Oil**—contains an aroma that supports the ability to forgive yourself and others while letting go of negative emotions, an important part of personal growth. Used for emotional support and energy balance.
>
> **Fulfill Your Destiny Essential Oil**—inhale during meditation or goal setting to support spiritual awareness. Diffuse before an important meeting or networking to create a grounded atmosphere.
>
> **Present-time Essential Oil**—used for empowerment; helps you focus on the here and now, so you can get beyond the past and move forward.
>
> **Surrender Essential Oil**—provide aromas to help cast off inhibitions that may be controlling your life or limiting your potential. Used for emotional balance.
>
> **Wise Men Essential Oil**—designed to promote feelings of reverence and spiritual awareness.
>
> **Oola Grow Essential Oil Blend**—gives you courage to focus on the task at hand and helps you move toward positive advancement and progression.
>
> **White Angelica Essential Oil**—use during yoga or meditation to create a positive and comforting atmosphere. You can create a positive atmosphere and inspire feelings of security and optimism no matter what life throws at you.
>
> **Valor Essential Oil**—use for empowerment, confidence, and energy balance.
>
> **Acceptance Essential Oil**—used for acceptance and self-worth; encourages feelings of self-worth.

Release Essential Oil—a blend that facilitates the ability to let go anger and frustration. Produces harmony and balance when diffused.

Sacred Frankincense Essential Oil—for those who wish to take their spiritual journey and meditation to a higher level.

The Gift Essential Oil—a blend of 7 ancient oils sought after for their calming properties.

Dream Catcher—used for spiritual awareness; to be able to chase after your dreams without the burden of negative thinking; use during meditation to promote inner strength; create an environment for emotional and spiritual grounding. This complex is ready to support you in your daily quest to catch your dreams.

Inner Child—used to encourage you to connect with your authentic self. Used for emotional balance.

These are actually mocking spirits operating through the philosophy of energy therapy—deceiving the non-discerning Christian to actually entertain them. Tragically, the truth is that Satan and his demons are being entertained by those who have opened their souls (mind, will, emotions) to them. The theory is that the oils through the olfactory process (smell) produce emotions. Christians have personally told me that certain oils bring back memories, and they feel the presence of the Holy Spirit. The Bible tells us to "test the spirits"! The Holy Spirit has no substitutes. The love of Jesus and the Cross of Calvary are inseparable from the Holy Spirit.

It is interesting in Mark 15:23, Jesus was offered wine drugged with myrrh to ease his pain on the Cross, but He refused it. Myrrh was given to those being crucified to ease the pain, making their death more bearable. That tells me that when Jesus said, "It is finished!" and I read that by His stripes I am healed—I know that He felt the fullness of all pain. He did not even take man's offer of numbness to alter His suffering for me. He was intentional about my salvation, healing, deliverance, and eternal life with Him. We were the joy set before Him. He knew raw, excruciating pain without a drug. *He did not alter His pain so why would He alter His plan?*

Again, each person must take responsibility for their own health. Knowing the body is the temple of the Holy Spirit and you have been purchased by God—you are not your own. I encourage people to go to websites and resources to check out products that are promoted as natural. Natural can mean many things to different people. From a healthcare professional, the word "natural" from a pure sense, connotes going back to the very basics: fresh air, sunlight, fresh water, healthy food, exercise, and quality sleep.

What Is Energy Healing?

Complementary Alternative Medicine (CAM), also called Natural Alternative and Complementary (NAC) therapies and holistic practices are prominent modalities that have appeared in the West. The American health system had primarily been dominated by a biomedical worldview. There has now been a paradigm shift for many that has reconceptualized health and healing to be holistic—body, mind, and spirit.

The concept of energy healing and its use as a philosophy for promoting holistic healing is not new. Energy therapies are ancient healing practices rooted in the belief that the body, mind, spirit, and emotions for a complex dynamic energy field can be manipulated to promote holistic healing (Popoola, M. 2015, pg. 39). The ultimate goal of CAM is not to promote healing but to induce or maintain a state of balance, harmony, and wholeness (body, mind, and spirit). Therefore, the understanding of the concepts of energy and holism are critical to understanding the holistic healing process and the management of stress-related diseases when these therapies are practiced (Popoola, 2015, pg. 39).

Holistic health is described from the National Center for Complementary and Integrative Health (NCCIH) as one who considers the whole person, including physical, mental, emotional, and spiritual aspects. Other concepts associated with holistic health by such organizations are energy, mind/body balance, spirit connection, physical wellness, emotional wellness, self-healing, traditional healing, and cultural healing (Popoola, M. 2015 pg.40). Unlike modern medical approaches, which are mechanical and fragmented in clinical care, holism is humanistic and always considers the environment, the culture, and the interconnections between other forms of life and energy on earth (Popoola, pg. 41).

As you can imagine—with these concepts and descriptions, holistic health opens itself to a world of many belief systems, conceptual frameworks, and religious traditions.

The NCCIH categorizes healing into categories: Natural, Mind-Body, or Traditional Healers.

- **Natural healing** reflects products such as herbs, vitamins, and minerals as dietary supplements.
- **Mind-Body healing** constitutes such things as yoga, meditation, massage therapy, acupuncture, tai-chi, qi-gong, healing touch, hypnotherapy, and yoga. Other places you may see prayer included in this category.
- **Traditional healing** include Ayurvedic medicine, Traditional Chinese medicine, homeopathy, and naturopathy.

In all of these except the natural dietary supplements, there is a spiritual component, many of which are called energy healing. As you can see from the description of essential oils as defined from *The Oils Used in the Bible* and the actual oil descriptions and uses from the previous chart, a spirituality or spiritual philosophy is inseparable and becomes much more than just a herb or dietary supplement.

Essential oils from some companies actually fit into holistic healing in the category of mind/body category, as well as the techniques such as raindrop therapy. Every energy therapy has an underlying philosophy interpreted to mean supernatural wisdom or spiritual consciousness that comes from God or Higher Self, packaged to the West in the form of health, wellness, or exercise. There are essential oil companies that are not just about promoting oils as a fragrance, beauty, or household product but about energy healing. They portray Jesus in their spiritual philosophy and relate the experiences as the Holy Spirit. The God consciousness that these philosophies are really promoting is a universal spiritually guided life force. The words life force, energy, and spirit are all used interchangeable; however, they all represent the demonic realm if it is not absolute biblical truth.

The Cross is missing! The Blood of Jesus is missing! The love and intimacy of the Father is missing! In Christian healing, the focus is on Christ, the Cross, and forgiveness of sins. The Gospel puts the focus of the ministry of Jesus as forgiveness of sins through His Cross.

People using these therapies with no understanding of truth are blindly following their leader or practitioner to select and promote a treatment plan for your condition. When using modalities that are intended for holistic healing, you are embracing the spirituality component behind the practice because it is intended to be inseparable. These health and wellness initiatives and practices have caused vulnerable people to open the doors to the occult. The spiritual experiences many claim to have is not the Holy Spirit. The reasons these trends of holism are accepted in the U.S. are because:

- Marketing implies that Reiki, Essential Oils, Therapeutic Touch and others are the same way Jesus healed.
- They satisfy the hunger for spirituality and transcendence.
- There are problems with allopathic (modern medicine), and people are seeking perceived improvements or alternatives.
- People desire more personal connections with their practitioner.
- People believe it is not God's will to heal everyone.

Healing Touch includes therapies like: Therapeutic Touch (TT), Reiki, shiatzu, reflexology, and raindrop technique. Christian laying on of hands for prayer is often lumped into this spiritual healing category—beware it is assimilated into all cultures with no reference to or belief in Calvary and the shed blood of Jesus Christ.

Therapeutic Touch (TT) is often considered the modern form of the ancient practice of laying on hands but it is done indirectly without touching but simply moving your hand over the body. TT, for example, is not considered a religion, but the practice has roots in ancient shamanism. I encourage you to research these various religions and practices and you will see and quickly understand the commonalities.

Even **Yoga** is a mind and body practice with origins in ancient Indian philosophy. Like other meditative movement practices, it has a distinct spiritual energy philosophy, along with posture and mantras.

There are many variations to "touch therapies" and "wellness movements" but the humanistic basic principle is to stimulate or change the energy channel of the body and help restore or maintain balance. What is disturbing about the healing power in these energy practices is that the power is the same life force behind occult practices that God abhors. The practice of Reiki actually uses mediums—one must be attuned or have energy channeled from a Master Reiki practitioner.

Hypnosis is a practice that puts a person in a state of sleep—a process with marked susceptibility to suggestion and considerable loss of will power and sensations. How frightening for a believer to intentionally surrender his will power to another person! Or for a person (hypnotherapist) to manipulate the thoughts of another human whom God created. Hypnotics are a class of drugs that produce sleep.

Yet those that practice these things have no difficulty ascribing the power to Jesus. The repackaging of false religions and ancient practices are intentional for Western audiences. The Bible is full of Scriptures with God's prohibition against trafficking in the spirit realm or using mediums. In all of these practices, we seem to have practitioners who profess to be Christ followers. Again, know what you are doing—guard your spiritual health—guard your relationship with Jesus! It is never acceptable to God to plug Jesus or His words into a pagan worldview to sanctify it as Christian.

When you come into the land that the Lord your God is giving you, you shall not learn to follow the abominable practices of those nations. There shall not be found among you anyone who burns his son or his daughter as an offering, anyone who practices divination or tells fortunes or interprets omens, or a sorcerer or a charmer or a medium or a necromancer or one who inquires of the dead, for whoever does these things is an abomination to the Lord. And because of these abominations the Lord your God is driving them out before you. You shall be blameless before the Lord your God, for these nations, which you are about to dispossess, listen to fortune-tellers and to diviners. But as for you, the Lord your God has not allowed you to do this.

I will raise up for them a prophet like you from among their brothers. And I will put my words in his mouth, and he shall speak to them all that I command him. And whoever will not listen to my words that he shall speak in my name, I myself will require it of him (Deuteronomy 18:9-14; 18-20).

In Christian healing, the focus is on Christ, the Cross, Christ's death and resurrection, and the fullness of walking in the Holy Spirit as we follow Jesus and His ways. The claims to practice essential oils or any other alternative health practice, such as yoga, therapeutic touch, or reflexology related to Jesus is absolutely false. The spirit, soul, and body yoking philosophy is not the Holy Spirit

Jesus said to him, "I am the way, and the truth, and the life. No one comes to the Father except through me" (John 14:6).

And when they could not get near him because of the crowd, they removed the roof above him, and when they had made an opening, they

let down the bed on which the paralytic lay. And when Jesus saw their faith, he said to the paralytic, "Son, your sins are forgiven." Now some of the scribes were sitting there, questioning in their hearts, "Why does this man speak like that? He is blaspheming! Who can forgive sins but God alone?" And immediately Jesus, perceiving in his spirit that they thus questioned within themselves, said to them, "Why do you question these things in your hearts? Which is easier, to say to the paralytic, 'Your sins are forgiven,' or to say, 'Rise, take up your bed and walk'? But that you may know that the Son of Man has authority on earth to forgive sins"—he said to the paralytic—"I say to you, rise, pick up your bed, and go home." And he rose and immediately picked up his bed and went out before them all, so that they were all amazed and glorified God, saying, "We never saw anything like this!" (Mark 2:4-12).

And the prayer of faith will save the one who is sick, and the Lord will raise him up. And if he has committed sins, he will be forgiven. Therefore, confess your sins to one another and pray for one another, that you may be healed. The prayer of a righteous person has great power as it is working (James 5:15-16).

Instead of condemning or accusing practitioners or participants—invite them to join you in becoming a disciple of Jesus. Begin to really minister to them the real Jesus, encouraging them to make Jesus Lord of their lives and loving them as Jesus did. Avoid seeing people as evil but simply a person with a different worldview. However, it is important for you to speak truth.

We Have An Enemy, but Who Is It?

I weep over the needless casualties of war of those who give up hope and take their own life—or give up just short of their miracle. Those that are incapacitated or tormented with chronic illness and are not walking in what God called them to do. Satan came to steal, kill, and destroy; he is stealing purpose and destinies, as well as taking out lives! If you follow Jesus, it is impossible to love God and not love people! We have an enemy. Satan and his demons are real.

For we do not wrestle against flesh and blood, but against the rulers, against the authorities, against the cosmic powers over this present darkness, against the spiritual forces of evil in the heavenly places (Ephesians 6:12).

The thief comes only to steal and kill and destroy. I came that they may have life and have it abundantly (John 10:10).

Now war arose in heaven, Michael and his angels fighting against the dragon. And the dragon and his angels fought back, but he was defeated, and there was no longer any place for them in heaven. And the great dragon was thrown down, that ancient serpent, who is called the devil and Satan, the deceiver of the whole world—he was thrown down to the earth, and his angels were thrown down with him. And I heard a loud voice in heaven, saying, "Now the salvation and the power and the kingdom of our God and the authority of his Christ have come, for the accuser of our brothers has been thrown down, who accuses them day and night before our God. And they have conquered him by the blood of the Lamb and by the word of their testimony, for they loved not their lives even unto death" (Revelation 12:7-11).

As Westerners, we struggle with the idea of the reality of an unseen realm, although we deal with the unseen realties of such things as cell phones and germs all the time. But when it comes to the spirit world, we totally ignore it or simply are entertained by it. The enemy is strategic.

So that we would not be outwitted by Satan; for we are not ignorant of his designs (2 Corinthians 2:11).

Satan will use deception. In other words he will disguise himself so that you will not at all recognize him or his demons. We don't need to know the names of demons or spirits, but we do need to realize their functions. For example, *Jealousy* (Numbers 5:14); *Heaviness* (Isaiah 61:3); *Fear* (2 Timothy 1:7); *Infirmity* (Luke

13:11). Many times we can identify the enemy because of how he is functioning: contrary to God's Word.

For God has not given us a spirit of fear, but of power and of love and of a sound mind (2 Timothy 1:7 NKJV).

And behold, there was a woman who had had a spirit of infirmity eighteen years, and she was bent over and could in no way raise herself up (Luke 13:11 NKJV).

And if the spirit of jealousy comes over him and he is jealous of his wife who has defiled herself, or if the spirit of jealousy comes over him and he is jealous of his wife, though she has not defiled herself (Numbers 5:14).

To console those who mourn in Zion, to give them beauty for ashes, the oil of gladness for mourning, the garment of praise instead for the spirit of heaviness; that they may be called trees of righteousness, the planting of the Lord, that He may be glorified (Isaiah 61:3 NKJV).

Satan works to pervert things and gain influence over our lives. The enemy's bottom line goals are:

- To seduce you to turn away from God and choose him.
- To hinder you from fulfilling what God has called and purposed you to do.
- To simply take you out!

There shall not be found among you anyone who makes his son or his daughter pass through fire, or one who practices witchcraft, or soothsayer, or one who interprets omens, or a sorcerer, or one who conjures up spells, or a medium, or a spiritist, or one who calls up the dead. For all who do these things are an abomination to the Lord, and because of these abominations the Lord your God drives them out before you (Deuteronomy 18:10-12 NKJV).

We give place to the enemy or open doors by things like occult involvement (Deut. 18:10-12), unforgiveness (Matt. 18:21-35), willful disobedience (Rom. 6:16; 1 Cor. 6:18; Gal. 5:19-20), or giving place to fear (Luke 12:32).

Pharaoh Has Been Challenged

Then Peter came up and said to him, "Lord, how often will my brother sin against me, and I forgive him? As many as seven times?" Jesus said to him, "I do not say to you seven times, but seventy-seven times. "Therefore the kingdom of heaven may be compared to a king who wished to settle accounts with his servants. When he began to settle, one was brought to him who owed him ten thousand talents. And since he could not pay, his master ordered him to be sold, with his wife and children and all that he had, and payment to be made. So the servant fell on his knees, imploring him, 'Have patience with me, and I will pay you everything.' And out of pity for him, the master of that servant released him and forgave him the debt. But when that same servant went out, he found one of his fellow servants who owed him a hundred denarii, and seizing him, he began to choke him, saying, 'Pay what you owe.' So his fellow servant fell down and pleaded with him, 'Have patience with me, and I will pay you.' He refused and went and put him in prison until he should pay the debt. When his fellow servants saw what had taken place, they were greatly distressed, and they went and reported to their master all that had taken place. Then his master summoned him and said to him, 'You wicked servant! I forgave you all that debt because you pleaded with me. And should not you have had mercy on your fellow servant, as I had mercy on you?' And in anger his master delivered him to the jailers, until he should pay all his debt. So also my heavenly Father will do to every one of you, if you do not forgive your brother from your heart" (Matthew 18:21-35).

Do you not know that if you present yourselves to anyone as obedient slaves, you are slaves of the one whom you obey, either of sin, which leads to death, or of obedience, which leads to righteousness? (Romans 6:16)

Flee from sexual immorality. Every other sin a person commits is outside the body, but the sexually immoral person sins against his own body (1 Corinthians 6:18).

Now the works of the flesh are evident: adultery, fornication, uncleanness, lewdness, idolatry, sorcery, hatred, contentions, jealousies, outbursts of wrath, selfish ambitions, dissension, heresies, envy, murders, drunkenness, revelries, and the like; of which I tell you beforehand, just as I also told you in time past, that those who practice such things will not inherit the kingdom of God. But the fruit of the Spirit is love, joy, peace, patience, kindness, goodness, faithfulness, gentleness, and self-control. Against such things there is no law. And those who are Christ's have crucified the flesh with its passions and desires. If we live by the Spirit, let us also walk in the Spirit. Let us not become conceited, provoking one another, envying one another (Galatians 5:19-26 NKJV).

When the enemy is operating in someone's life, he is causing torment, struggle, and anxiety as examples of strategies. When we give place to the enemy, we are giving him permission instead of the legitimate operation of the Holy Spirit.

The discipleship process is important. Our identity in Christ and what Jesus completed at the cross become our focus, not the enemy! Biblical healing and freedom are about receiving God's grace and the fullness of God's presence in us to become who God created and redeemed us to be. I do not give the enemy a platform or much attention at all. I choose Jesus.

We have been conditioned that evil (death) and good are opposing forces—they both came from the same tree. We then try to restrain evil. We make choices from the lens of what is good or what is bad. Instead, the right question to ask is, "What produces life?" If you receive the breath of God—the Holy Spirit—you bring the presence of God. You bring love and peace that replaces fear and hate.

The human will is not to choose between good and evil but designed to choose God as your Source and not self or another source. Your source of truth will drive you. The bottom line is that anything outside of Jesus is humanism; perversion of Jesus is not God. Any stronghold is idolatry. God wants to be the center of truth in your life. God is jealous! Anytime God says one thing and

I believe what the enemy says, I place Satan in the center of truth in my life. Anytime we believe lies, we place our security in other things. Essentially, we are saying to God, "I will take it from here!" Many things we cannot control. However, we choose, who is our source. We have freedom to change sources at any time.

Occult Involvement

Occult involvement is forbidden by the Lord (Deuteronomy 18:9-14). Satan will offer counterfeit access to the spiritual realm. His points of access are seducing, and most enter naively because people have no knowledge of the practices in which they enter or no knowledge of God's Word. Satan is subtle when he says, "It's just a game" about ouija boards, Pokémon, horoscopes, carnival fortune tellers, mediums, and magic. "Oh it's just harmless fun or an alternative therapy, right?" Or, "It's just a movie so it's just pretend or make believe." How many times do you hear rationalization or justification to what the Holy Spirit is speaking to you to question or judge? Be aware of the Holy Spirit nudging or creating something unsettling in your spirit. He is the greatest Teacher if we allow Him to teach and counsel the whole word of God.

Ask the Holy Spirit to teach you what you need to know related specifically to occult exposure in your own life. God is speaking—ask Him, He will show you any changes you need to make for your own life. There are many occult practices. There is hidden spirituality behind many alternative health practices for healing and wellness. Any secret societies or associations (Free Masons), satanic practices (Dungeons and Dragons), false religions, secret initiations, and oaths. Any ceremony or covenant required by any other source is also a red flag. We are to receive guidance only from the Word of God.

The World Is Watching! America's Theological Shift to Religious Pluralism

Professor of Religious Studies at Indiana University, Candy Gunter Brown, wrote a book based on her nine-year research findings from a national project involving our religious culture. She wrote from a cultural and religious historian perspective because she found the mainstreaming of Complementary Alternative Medicine (CAM) to have a remarkable progression in our country. Dr. Brown introduced her project by saying she stumbled upon it when interviewing Pentecostals about divine healing practices. She was surprised by the number of people who volunteered information regarding their love for Complementary Alternative Medicine (CAM). Popular names for CAM today are holistic, complementary, alternative, integrative, and mind/body practices.

The book reveals the history of how health care practices, which once were thought to be medically and religiously not legitimate, are becoming integrated into secular, and particularly, Christian settings. They used to be categorized as not legitimate mainly because of their goal of achieving harmony with life-force energy, which is a universal religious philosophy considered New Age. CAM now seems right for everyone.

Dr. Brown (2013) described singling out Evangelicals and other conservative Christians as a case study, although other cultural groups could have been selected, because she considered Evangelicals to be a barometer for the mainstreaming of a once marginal cultural practice. She described Evangelicals as "culturally adaptive biblical experientialist" who seek a transformational presence in culture while maintaining biblical standards of purity. She further described them as the Christians who appropriate non-Christian resources from their surrounding cultures to evangelize and edify believers but who also use the Bible to safeguard against cultural blending.

Pharaoh Has Been Challenged

The book explains how and why CAM entered into America's cultural mainstream, gained a foothold into the Evangelical and other theological conservative Christian lifestyles and beliefs when most of CAM is religious, but non-Christian, and lacks scientific evidence, efficacy, and safety. Evangelicals would not usually endorse religious combinations because it would be construed as idolatrous worship of other gods. However, Dr. Brown points out that these are the same people who seem to have embraced the healing practices rooted in and byproducts of metaphysical religion by conceptually reclassifying these practices from New Age to that of science. She does not make a claim to what Christians or other Americans should believe or practice, but asked the question, "What happens when people transpose religious and secular categories?" She concludes by voicing her concern about the processes and context in which CAM has been mainstreamed and is being promoted because the mechanisms affect decisions about health and religious beliefs.

She described the evangelical and other conservative Christian subgroup as many people with unmet health needs and physical and emotional suffering with repeated attempts and failures to find help from traditional medical or religious resources. Dr. Brown described evidence that experimenting with any CAM approach can be a gateway to holistic or metaphysical spirituality worldviews and that people who engage or participate in them are more than likely to unintentionally change their theological orientation.

As a born-again Christ follower, I realized these findings validated what the Lord had already been showing me and my own personal observations in healthcare. *Calling the Church out of Egypt* is a glimpse into what the world sees regarding those professing to know Jesus Christ. It is insight into what non-Christian cultures describe us to be—definitely not set apart and making the God of Abraham known. It is from this anguish in prayer that Zoe Healing Center vision was birthed and the Lord has given me the words in this book and the urgency to share them for such a time as this.

Because Christians do, indeed, define their religious beliefs in terms of intellectual creeds and statements of faith, rather than body/mind rituals, many don't recognize the practices such as Yoga, acupuncture and acupressure, Reiki, Therapeutic Touch, Transcendental Meditation or Mindfulness, psychophysiology, chiropractic, martial arts, aromatherapy (essential oils), or any mind/body CAM practice or therapy as a universal or metaphysical spirituality. Dr. Brown described the incidences of the adverse negative effects of the vital force or energy practices, such as insanity, violence, and mental breakdown with practices such as meditation and yoga kundalini energy experiences, as well as physical things such as stroke with chiropractic treatments.

Mind, Body, and Spirit

The concepts of mind, spirit, and flesh are inseparable because holistic health, in contrast to traditional medicine, presupposes that all reality is essentially one (monism), thus matter and energy, physical and nonphysical entities, exist in a continuum and constantly affect each other. We view the words, mind, body, and spirit, as a common phrase in our society.

What is alarming to me is that people don't know, especially professing Christians, or they don't notice the significance of the term "spirit." Spirit as in spirituality, means that humans are perceived to be spiritual living beings beyond the physical life, therefore, the term metaphysical. The concepts are interpreted as communicating between natural and spiritual realms, psychic intuition, and using nonmaterial energy to change the material world.

A central assumption running through the diverse CAM practices is the existence and possibility of redirecting universal life force or "vital energy." The energy can be called by many names such as qi (chee), ki, prana, animal magnetism, vital force, biofields, and Innate Intelligence. Actually this concept is already familiar to most people as it was introduced as "the force" in Star Wars. It is easy to gloss over these terms and not recognize there is a spirit behind them.

Vital energy is more than a physical force or a general term without contradiction. In a holistic worldview, vital energy is considered alive and life-giving, intelligent and goal directed, and purposed to bring homeostasis or balance. It is subtle, meaning it cannot be proven; therefore, people claim to know it is real by intuition or observation of apparent effects. Dr. Browns' descriptions, historical detail, and case studies within each of these practices make this book a great resource for Christians who want to make informed decisions before giving consent to participate or endorsing these practices.

Summary of Observations and Behaviors of Evangelical and Other Theological Subcultures as Described in "America's Healing Gods" (Brown, 2013). I find it interesting and an opportunity to educate people as we make disciples and pray more specifically for those distressed who desire healing.

- CAM stresses natural, scientifically validated benefits. Whether or not you are told, practices are founded on assumptions from multiple religious traditions such as Buddhism, Hinduism, Taoism, and metaphysics spirituality.
- CAM providers strategically marketed as effective and wholesome therapies and repackaged them as non-religious health care, fitness, scientific techniques, and psychology tools to enhance human performance. Because the contemporary language used is congruent with popular science such as quantum physics and neuroscience, rather than religious rituals, the spiritual philosophy has been recast to be in accord with evangelicals and other conservative Christians, as "good fruit."

- Evangelical Christians will guard against theological contamination while appropriating non-Christian resources for Christian resources.
- The good fruit is considered religiously neutral science; therefore has made evangelical Christians more likely to use practices premised in a non-Christian worldview and without realizing it, leading to theological shifts.
- Christians talk about the danger of national judgment and losing the blessings of God because political leaders support abortion, same-sex marriage, Islam, and New Age, all of which correspond to idolatry in Egypt and Old Testament practices. But all the while they never acknowledge the gods of health which they are invoking. Is this pleasing to God?
- Pain relief, benefits of health, and deeper spiritual experiences overrule one's theological doctrine, beliefs, or creed. Man's flesh and desires will rule over theology.
- Reason or rationality will trump theological beliefs in order for a Christian to attempt to keep that identity. In other words, it is not a problem to compromise and still be a Christian.
- Because Christians don't stand up to criticism to defend their beliefs, but instead will modify or make a counterfeit Christian version.
- Using contemporary scientific language, metaphysical practices are promoted as a superior form of medicine and fill the gap that medicine and religion cannot fill.
- Holistic providers have done more to investigate and alleviate Christian concerns than Christians have done to investigate CAM. These monistic worldviews promote nonspecific spiritual interventions and are comparable to all religious traditions.

As a Christian, it is easier to discern the deception as it comes when one is informed regarding its source of truth and why things are purposed to work. Even though historically, the Pentecostal movement rejected cessationism and there was a renewed expectation for miracles, there is still much confusion and fragmentation today among and within denominations and other "Christian" subcultures and clergy. Many Christian denominations believe in cessationism, live in unbelief that God is the same today, or if it is even His will to heal. All of this has discouraged people of expecting any miracles and is pushing people to reason that they should pursue anything they can find that works.

How can we be pleasing to God when we profess to be born-again, spirit-filled Christ followers and piece together and blend multiple sources of worldviews to ease our pain and suffering or supply our needs? In Romans 8:6 God says to be carnally minded (flesh, five senses) is death, but to be spiritually minded is life and peace.

> *For those who live according to the flesh set their minds on the things of the flesh, but those who live according to the Spirit, the things of the Spirit. For to be carnally minded is death, but to be spiritually minded is life and peace. Because the carnal mind is enmity against God; for it is not subject to the law of God, nor indeed can be. So then those who are in the flesh cannot please God. But you are not in the flesh, but of the Spirit, if indeed the Spirit of God dwells in you. Now if anyone does not have the Spirit of Christ, he is not His* (Romans 8:5-9 NKJV).

> *But if the Spirit of Him who raised Jesus from the dead dwells in you, He who raised Christ from the dead will also give life to your mortal bodies through His Spirit who dwells in you* (Romans 8:11 NKJV).

Ashamed of the Gospel?

To me, the bottom line for us Christians is that we ignore the source of Life (Genesis 2:7). We are ashamed of the Gospel of

Jesus Christ, or we simply don't have a relationship with Jesus Christ. Are you really born-again? Just like the Holy Spirit cannot be separated from Jesus Christ and His redemptive work on the cross, paying our debt for sin, any other spirit is from the realm of darkness and is demonic. The demonic spirit that is associated with these holistic metaphysical spirituality practices cannot be separated from the false doctrine it represents. There are no substitutions for the Holy Spirit. Call it what it is: religious pluralism. Religious pluralism is not pleasing to God and will not be tolerated. God calls any other doctrine cursed (Galatians 1:8-9).

And the LORD God formed man of the dust of the ground, and breathed into his nostrils the breath of life; and man became a living being (Genesis 2:7 NKJV).

But even if we, or an angel from heaven, preach any other gospel to you than what we have preached to you, let him be accursed. As we have said before, so now I say again, if anyone preaches any other gospel to you than what you have received, let him be accursed (Genesis 1:8-9 NKJV).

Live Loved; Live Well; Live Him!

I am not ashamed of the Gospel of Christ because it is the power of God to salvation for everyone who believes (Romans 1:16-17). I trust the power of God's words. I will not be afraid to seek and trust the Kingdom of God first. When difficulties come, my God will make a way (Hebrews 13:8, Romans 5:1-2). Ask the Holy Spirit to discern those things that are contrary to God's Word. God is serious about what He says, and He is faithful to do what He says. Psalm 103 reminds us God says He will be our Savior, Healer, Deliver, and Provider—we must choose Him through Jesus Christ.

For I am not ashamed of the gospel of Christ, for it is the power of God to salvation for everyone who believes, for the Jew first and also for the Greek. 17 For in it the righteousness of God is revealed from faith to faith; as it is written, "The just shall live by faith" (Romans 1:16-17 NKJV)

Jesus Christ is the same yesterday, today, and forever (Hebrews 13:8 NKJV).

Therefore, having been justified by faith, we have peace with God through our Lord Jesus Christ, 2 through whom also we have access by faith into this grace in which we stand, and rejoice in hope of the glory of God (Romans 5:1-2 NKJV).

Bless the Lord, O my soul, and forget not all His benefits: 3) Who forgives all your iniquities, who heals all your diseases, 4) who redeems your life from destruction, who crowns you with lovingkindness and tender mercies (Psalm 103:2-4 NKJV).

The things which you learned and received and heard and saw in me, these do, and the God of peace will be with you (Philippians 4:9 NKJV).

Renounce your participation in these practices, turn from them, and receive salvation. Acts 4:12 says there is no salvation in any other name under heaven given among men by which we must be saved. (Grk. *sozo* Strong's #4982—save, heal, preserve, rescue, restore, deliver, make whole).

Nor is there salvation in any other name under heaven given among men by which we must be saved (Acts 4:12 NKJV).

The word "other" (Grk. *heteros*, Strong's #2087) means a different generic distinction, another kind, not of the same nature, form, or class. Here, *heteros* denotes a distinction and an exclusivity, with no second choices, or opinions. Jesus, You are the only One—there is no heteros, no other (*World Wealth, New Spirit Filled Living Bible*, NKJV).

Whatever the issue, the answer is always the same—JESUS! Jesus said that it is His Spirit who gives life and "The words that I speak to you are spirit and are life. But there are some of you who do not believe" (John 6:63-64). Victory is Jesus; Healing is Jesus; Freedom is Jesus; Life is Jesus! He is the Word. Trust Him!

Receive Freedom

Receive freedom by first acknowledging it and then *repent*. You will not fulfill your destiny until you are delivered. Free people free people.

1. Repent—turn away from it.
2. Renounce any previous or current involvement.
3. Ask Jesus to forgive you for engaging in the activity and to take His place as Lord of your life.
4. Command any anti-Christ spirits to go in Jesus' name.
5. Ask Jesus to fill you up with the Holy Spirit and receive Him.

Fear

We will respond to fear by what we believe:

Forget **E**verything **A**nd **R**un

or

False **E**vidence **A**ppearing **R**eal

I sought the Lord, and He heard me and delivered me from all my fears (Psalm 34:4).

It is easy to begin to worship the opposite of what we fear. For example, if you fear rejection, you become focused and obsessed about being accepted or a need to belong. Fears are often rooted in the fear of death. For example, people are not afraid of heights—they are afraid of falling to their death. Water—fear of drowning; darkness—fear of what they can't see might harm them.

As we get closer to God, the less we should fear death. Three most common fears that drive our lives are: fear of death, rejection, and failure. In His Word, God addresses every fear and challenge we would ever face in this world. When we have irrational fear, we need revelation from God.

Fear can also be a demonic spirit such as Paul addressed in 2 Timothy 1:7 (NKJV),

For God has not given us a spirit of fear, but of power, and of love, and of a sound mind.

God does not want us to be ignorant of the devices of Satan. That is why we need the Holy Spirit and His discernment to identify the enemy's gains and entrances in our lives.

Rational fear is a sensible, cautious fear that God gave us to keep us safe. It is a natural response of our defense mechanism so we can be alert and respond quickly. Irrational fear is a fear without reason or understanding. This fear is based on illusions and false beliefs. These are lies that keep us from fulfilling God's plan for our lives. These false beliefs must be exposed, rooted out, and replaced by the truth of God's Word and the very presence of God Himself.

For Christians, fear demonstrates itself when we are asking ourselves, "What if God doesn't heal me?" Oh but He did! "What if He doesn't protect me or provide for me?" I believe fear is what the enemy is using to paralyze the body of Christ, keeping people from following the command to "Go, make disciples." It is the reason why people are stuck in unbelief that drives and motivates them and fall into disobedience and idolatry. Fear is why we run to every treatment that might promise a cure or better quality of life; it is why we accept drugs and treatments all the while knowing there are huge risks involved. Fear is why we run to secular counselors and don't lay hands on the sick. Fear is why we don't share our testimony or Christ's love in the marketplace. Fear of death, fear of rejection, fear of failure. Holy Spirit, we really, really need you!

Possessing God's love results in fearless confidence towards God. It's the love of God that casts out all fear. That is why we need the Holy Spirit's presence in our lives. Having an intimate relationship with our Father God, knowing His nature, His will, and His love for you surpasses anything you can imagine!

> *There is no fear in love; but perfect love casts out all fear, because fear involves torment. But he who fears has not been made perfect in love* (1 John 4:18).

Jesus also linked fear to lack of faith. When the disciples entered a storm in Matthew 8:26, Jesus asked, "Why are you fearful, O you of little faith?" Jesus was confident in the Father's love and His Kingdom authority, but He also possessed the very nature of God. Abba Father, I want to come to know You so completely!

> *The fear of the Lord is the beginning of wisdom* (Proverbs 9:10).

One of the many facets of the Holy Spirit is wisdom and understanding.

> *There shall come forth a shoot from the stump of Jesse, and a branch from his roots shall bear fruit. And the Spirit of the Lord shall rest upon him, the Spirit of wisdom and understanding, the Spirit of counsel and might, the Spirit of knowledge and the fear of the Lord. And his delight shall be in the fear of the Lord* (Isaiah 11:1-3).

When we truly understand who God is and who we are in Him—when we truly understand that God is so much greater than any problem, situation, infirmity, circumstance, or Satan himself—we can be confident that our source of Life is God and Him alone, in Jesus' name!

Whom will you fear? A righteous fear of God and being filled with God Himself should have dominion over every other fear in your life.

> *Behold, I have given you authority to tread on serpents and scorpions, and over all the power of the enemy, and nothing shall hurt you* (Luke 10:19).

Each person is created in God's own image. We are seeing so

many spiritual influences of the enemy—alcohol, drugs (whether illegal or legal mind altering) in our culture today. We are so busy trying to label and manage by conventional humanism philosophies, but spiritual conditions require spiritual answers. We need to address the spiritual condition of people and call it what it is—sin caused by demonic influences.

Jesus is the only answer—the only way! Jesus tells us to heal the sick and cast out demons! When a person understands that freedom is not the bondage of something but stepping into the presence of Someone—Jesus—life radically changes. One encounter with Jesus, one word from the Lord changes everything. People can turn around to follow Jesus. Without Him, we are stuck in a cycle of defeat—spinning away from God—lost, dying, and eternally separated from God to a place called hell. God's will is that for each person to be dependent on Him and nothing or no one else! His commandment stands, "No other gods before Me!"

I am the vine; you are the branches. Whoever abides in me and I in him, he it is that bears much fruit, for apart from me you can do nothing (John 15:5).

I beseech you therefore, brethren, by the mercies of God, that you present your bodies a living sacrifice, holy, acceptable to God, which is your reasonable service. And do not be conformed to this world, but be transformed by the renewing of your mind, that you may prove what is that good and acceptable and perfect will of God (Romans 12:1-2 NKJV).

Psychology: Science or Religion?

Because of our widespread embrace of syncretism, I believe we have made psychology sacred by endorsing humanistic philosophies blended with our Christian beliefs. In addition, I agree with those that also believe we have embraced secular psychology as a religion by attempting to blend and overlay biblical principles onto a humanism foundation. The result is chaos, confusion, hopelessness, and death. We have embraced and brought psychology into the belief systems and lifestyle of believers and into the church. Psychology is humanism and does not mix with the Holy Spirit. Psychology is everywhere among Christian organizations and institutions—books and other types of literature formats, direct referrals from clergy, screening of missionaries, leadership coaching, and even sermons.

It is interesting that as secular psychology researchers are publishing controversy and lack of confidence in psychological counseling and drug therapy, professing Christians are pursuing it. Christian counseling centers are multiplying and offering what many believe is the perfect combination of Christianity and Psychology.

Christians perceive psychology counselors to be experts for advice on how to become emotionally stable, how to better organize themselves, how to set goals, how to communicate better, how to better relate to each other in marriage, how to face the challenges of life, and in actuality—how to treat their soul issues (will, mind, and emotions). Wow! From a first century Spirit-filled Christ follower's perspective, these are symptoms of a life without Christ, a life void of the fullness of God operating in and through them as witnesses of a risen Jesus. When we can have the God of the universe and His advice and counsel on all things that pertain to the affairs of man, why would we settle for less? Why would we go back to Egypt in pursue of other gods?

I sound so repetitive, but it all goes back to taking responsibility for your spiritual growth and maturity, and your own health and wellness. It doesn't take long to research to whom and what you are surrendering your body, soul, and spirit!

One great resource for Christians, is *Anatomy of an Epidemic: Psychiatric Drugs and the Astonishing Rise of Mental Health Illness in America* (Whitaker, D. 2005). I already speculated the conclusions of these research findings, based on my personal observation of patients and trends in my own career in healthcare. I am so glad to see scientific evidence-based findings and psychiatrists themselves publishing their recommendations against this huge industry that contributes to death rather than life.

According to this particular article, the modern era of psychopharmacology was born in 1955 with the wonder drug—an anti-psychotic, Thorazine. Following quickly were other meds which began the rise of mental illnesses in this country. Of course there are now second-generation drugs, but the effects are the same. This author reports that the review of scientific literature reveals that it is our drug-based paradigm of care that is fueling this epidemic.

The drugs make things worse. The drugs increase the likelihood that a person will become chronically ill, and they induce new and more severe psychiatric symptoms in a significant percentage of patients. He reports that drug after drug actually changes the brain chemistry when the public has been told that it is the brain chemistry that is out of balance and requires restoration. Lastly, he reports from the findings that there are greater fatalities, mental health symptoms, increased violence, and insane behavior, disabilities, and chronic illness (Whitaker, 2005).

Wow! *Is it really worth the risk?* They say there are no cures! With my spiritual eyes, I see the enemy abducting vulnerable Christians, wandering from a Shepherd and spinning in a downward spiral towards a death trap.

Again, we need the Holy Spirit! I have simplified my life. I believe in the simplicity and truth of the Gospel of Jesus Christ. God has never failed me. Jesus is enough! His blood has never lost its power. His name is above all names, labels, and lies; all must bow to His Kingdom authority. His Word is life and will totally transform you!

> *The sorrows of those who run after another god shall multiply; their drink offerings of blood I will not pour out or take their names on my*

lips (Psalm 16:4).

Like the Psalmist in Psalm 23 says, "He restores my soul" (will, mind, and emotions). We need to take an active part in our relationship with God and learn to quiet our soul in His presence by renewing our mind and watching Him do the supernatural.

But I have calmed and quieted my soul, like a weaned child with its mother; like a weaned child is my soul within me (Psalm 131:2).

The Lord is my shepherd; I shall not want. He makes me lie down in green pastures. He leads me beside still waters. He restores my soul. He leads me in paths of righteousness for his name's sake. Even though I walk through the valley of the shadow of death, I will fear no evil, for you are with me; your rod and your staff, they comfort me.

You prepare a table before me in the presence of my enemies; you anoint my head with oil; my cup overflows. Surely goodness and mercy shall follow me all the days of my life, and I shall dwell in the house of the Lord forever (Psalm 23:1-6).

I wait for the Lord, my soul waits, and in His word I do hope (Psalm 130:5).

The Lord will perfect that which concerns me; Your mercy, O Lord, endures forever; Do not forsake the works of Your hands (Psalm 138:8 NKJV).

Healthcare is a prominent area of practice. People in this field are the most compassionate and respected individuals that I know. Most professionals have a desire to see people get well and to improve their quality of life. Again, this information is never intended to accuse or slander people. It is an attempt to open the eyes of understanding for those that profess to follow Christ. I believe God is calling people once again back to Himself. Can Jesus really be enough? Can you imagine every clinical person in psychology professing Jesus is enough? Can you imagine the miracles and testimonies we would see? Is it fear or unbelief that is hindering you?

Yes, it will cost! Yes, some would lose their jobs, maybe licenses. Some are now allowing the Holy Spirit to guide them with clients, as well as navigate their career.

Psychology is subtle but is widespread as it has quickly permeated the whole body of Christ. The sheep are starving and wandering, and don't even know it. Psychology, like so many other humanism modalities, promises far more than it can deliver; and what it does deliver is not the spiritual truth/food that nourishes and promotes spiritual growth. It causes confusion and dependents, not disciples. It is problem focused, not promise confident. It leads to further compromise and hopelessness, not life. Yet, even ministers perceive psychology with respect and awe and forget the God that heals and sets people free—His wonderful works towards man.

Another great resource on this subject is *Psycho Heresy: The Psychological Seduction of Christianity* (Bobgan and Bobgan, 2012). These authors detail a comprehensive history and literature review of psychology, practices, and famous Christian psychologists who contributed to the introduction of these practices and tools into the church. Let the Holy Spirit speak to you with the standard of God's Word.

There are generally four myths about psychology which have now become the cultural standard for Christianity (Bobgan and Bobgan 2012):

Myth 1: Psychotherapy (psychologic counseling along with its theories and techniques) is a science based on empirical evidence gleaned from measurable and consistent data. (In actuality, psychology is considered by many professionals as "pseudoscience.")

Myth 2: The best kind of counseling utilizes both psychology and the Bible. Psychologists or counselors who claim to be Christians generally say that they are more qualified to help people understand themselves and their behavior than other Christians, which include pastors who are not trained in psychology.

Myth 3: People who are experiencing mental/emotional/behavioral problems are mentally ill. They are psychologically sick. Therefore, ministers treat the spirit, psychologists treat the mind and emotions, and doctors treat the body. Anyone else is unqualified. (Does this even remotely resemble the Book of Acts?)

Myth 4: Psychotherapy has a high rate of success. It is seen as more effective than biblical counseling in helping people. That is one reason why so many Christians are going into this profession. Jesus is no longer front and center—in fact, God is not more qualified than the counselor. (Tragically, Jesus is no longer front and center—in fact, God is less qualified than the counselor!)

Jesus didn't come to pardon bad behavior, He came to offer us the gift of LIFE. Through a relationship with Christ, He transforms not what we think but how we think, and righteous fruit grows—love, joy, peace, longsuffering, kindness, goodness, faithfulness, gentleness, and self-control.

In my opinion, the fact that psychology, which was purposed only to describe human behavior, has crossed the line in now trying to explain it and change it. They have gone from description to prescription; moved from science to man's opinions. The dark origin of psychology was discussed earlier. Satan has always wanted to be God and possess the human soul. It was such a tragic day in history when the priests turned over the souls of men to psychiatry.

And the Lord said: "Because this people draw near with their mouth and honor me with their lips, while their hearts are far from me, and their fear of me is a commandment taught by men" (Isaiah 29:13).

Bobgan and Bobgan (2012) cite many studies where psychology has been opinioned a pseudoscience, resting on false premises (opinions, guesses, subjective explanations) and leading to false and sometimes harmful conclusions. A pseudoscience is a system of theories, assumptions, and methods that are erroneously regarded as scientific. Pseudoscience will use scientific labels to protect and promote opinions that can neither be proved nor refuted.

The actual foundation of psychotherapy are various philosophical humanism worldviews: determinism, existentialism, and even evolutionism (Bobgan 2012). World renowned psychiatrist E. Fuller Torry compared the techniques used by Western psychiatrists, with few exceptions, as being on exactly the same scientific plane as those with witchdoctors (Bobgan and Bobgan 2012).

Psychology is attempting to address the issues of life so that a person can live life with quality, civility, and effectiveness as a contributing member of society. Psychology addresses the same things that concern God; however, He has already addressed these instructions and promises in Scripture. Since God's Word already tells us how to live, how to change behavioral issues, and teaches attitudes and values, psychology is viewed as a religion. Carl Jung (Father of Psychoanalysis) stated it this way,

> Religions are systems of healthy psychic illness… that is why patients force psychotherapists into the role of priest, and expect and demand of him that he shall free them from their distress. That is why we psychotherapists must occupy ourselves with problems, which strictly speaking, belong to the theologian (Bobgan and Bobgan, 2012, pg. 131).

Psychiatrist Thomas Szasz describes human relations, called psychotherapy, are matters of religion. He further perceives that human relations are mislabeled "therapeutic" at great risk to our spiritual well-being. He then further describes psychotherapy as a fake religion that seeks to destroy true religion. It has a modern scientific sounding name for what used to be "cure of (sinful) souls." The cure of sinful souls used to be addressed as part of Christian religions but have been recast as cure of (sick) minds and became an integral part of medicine (Bobgan and Bobgan, 2012).

This description from Dr. Szasz for the cure of sick souls, sounds like it was once a vital mission of the church. I see it as the Great Commission—go make disciples, teaching them to observe everything Jesus taught us! There are complications of counterfeit gospels and false religions. Whom are you serving? Whom do you choose? Who is your source of Truth? It is not about choosing good or evil (remember both are from same tree and both lead to destruction), it is about choosing Life! It's not too late—Come, Jesus is calling!

> *And Jesus came and said to them, "All authority in heaven and on earth has been given to me. Go therefore and make disciples of all nations, baptizing them in the name of the Father and of the Son and of the Holy Spirit, teaching them to observe all that I have commanded you. And behold, I am with you always, to the end of the age"* (Matthew 28:18-20).

Thank God that He has brought healing and freedom ministries back into communities. Many church leaders contend that the church doesn't have the ability to meet the needs of people suffering from depression, anxiety, fear, and other problems. Yet this results in another open door for the enemy to gain access and torment to the vulnerable.

Through psychology, another type of spirituality can also be easily introduced. This is sometimes called **transpersonal psychology** which does involve faith and the supernatural—something beyond the physical universe. The spirituality in these settings offer mystical experiences of both the occult and esoteric and Eastern religions. These are actually foreign religions entering into the West in psychology language. The deception is now causing Western psychologists to look to Eastern cultures as having a better understanding of the human mind and emotions than what we have in the West (Gogban, and Gogban, 2012). People are searching for the supernatural!

In summary, psychology does not seem to be what many think it is, thus they place their trust in philosophies instead of God. There are several points to ponder when considering Christian psychology as an intervention for Christians or career path:

- Since its existence, there is no clear standardization in practices. Christian counselors can pick from many tools and techniques and can decide for himself/herself which opinions or conceptual frameworks to use. The Bible contains only the pure truth. All other truth is distorted by the limitations of human perception.
- We now seem to equate psychology and theology through semantic deception. Syncretism has permeated and is accepted and is promoted as acceptable to God.
- The Gospel of Self is another gospel according to the Bible. Popular themes of self-fulfillment, self-actualization, and self-worth. These teachings are products of humanism. According to Bobgan and Bobgan (2012), these are merely more palatable words to be relevant and avoid confessing sin, ungodly living, and lack of discipline.

Do Not Go Down to Egypt

"Ah, stubborn children," declares the Lord, "who carry out a plan, but not mine, and who make an alliance, but not of my Spirit, that they may add sin to sin (Isaiah 30:1).

What has happened is because so many ministers desired to Christianize psychology, we now have psychologized Christianity. Is this the church for which Christ is soon returning? Is the Bride ready? I don't believe so. The good news is that He is giving us time to repent from spiritual adultery and idolatry!

God has chosen us—He set His love upon us because of who He is. When we become believers, His love, His power, His identity and forgiveness, our worth, our esteem, and our acceptance are because of Him and His grace! That is the powerful message of the Gospel of Jesus Christ that never gets old or irrelevant. It is only through the blood of Jesus that we can receive our sight again and be whole!

God sees it all and is true and faithful. I believe He is bringing everything to a close soon. I believe He is hearing the cries of His people in torment and distress, especially those that have been led astray into snares or do not have a voice in their own decisions. God is setting us up so that His glory can be revealed. The whole world will see that people don't need psychology or anything else but Him! The world needs Jesus. Freedom is Truth—a Person, Jesus! Continue to pray for pastors and leaders. Pray for the Church to take God's Word seriously because He does mean what He says. Pray that all those professing to be Christians will become fully-devoted disciples of Jesus Christ, trusting and obeying His every Word. The Words that He speaks are Spirit and Life! (1 John 6:63).

You Will Not Abandon My Soul

Preserve me, O God, for in you I take refuge. I say to the Lord, "You are my Lord; I have no good apart from you." As for the saints in the land, they are the excellent ones, in whom is all my delight. The sorrows of those who run after another god shall multiply; their drink offerings of blood I will not pour out or take their names on my lips. The Lord is my chosen portion and my cup; you hold my lot. The lines have fallen for me in pleasant places; indeed, I have a beautiful inheritance.

I bless the Lord who gives me counsel; in the night also my heart instructs me. I have set the Lord always before me; because he is at my right hand, I shall not be shaken. Therefore my heart is glad, and my whole being rejoices; my flesh also dwells secure. For you will not abandon my soul to Sheol, or let your holy one see corruption. You make known to me the path of life; in your presence there is fullness of joy; at your right hand are pleasures forevermore (Psalm 16:1-11).

What a picture of intimacy! Everything goes back to a Father that loves and enables us to do something humanly impossible. Even my faith is a gift. Everything in us happens because of His Grace. You can't love God and not love people. Call out the gold in people—recognize the excellence in them—God does! Pray for those that do not have intimate knowledge and relationship with God. Share what Jesus has done for you! You witness of His love and greatness through a testimony. The world is waiting!

Time Is of the Essence—Come Out of Egypt

God continues to speak—to draw people back to Himself through His Word and goodness and mercy. Today, just like yesterday, people did not attend to the Words of the Lord. People ignored God's instructions and hated discipline.

God is offering us Wisdom—Himself—to navigate in the last days and to be the witness Jesus intended us to be. He is calling His Church—His body of believers that love Him and are attentive to hear and obey Him.

David Wilkerson called it the "Remnant"—God's called out ones—a Samuel Company. Those who will say, "Here I am, Lord, I am listening!" We choose. God has given each person a choice. Is His Bride ready? Only you can answer that question. Jesus is coming very soon. Only those who are ready and eagerly watching for His return will go to meet Him in the air. In the meantime, we are to be zealously and faithfully about the Father's business, preaching the Word and making disciples. One more soul, Lord, one more!

We ask, "What shall we do?" just as the people were asking Peter at Pentecost. The same passage applies to us today.

> *And Peter said to them, "Repent and be baptized every one of you in the name of Jesus Christ for the forgiveness of your sins, and you will receive the gift of the Holy Spirit"* (Acts 2:38).

Second Chronicles 20:1-30 is known for King Jehoshaphat's prayer. These passages explain how the Lord grants victory to those who trust Him. Jehoshaphat was facing a great threat to him and his country during his reign. Great multitudes were coming against them. Against incredible odds in what seemed a hopeless situation, Jehoshaphat humbled himself before the Lord. Then he trusted what God said and saw a mighty victory. When he heard the news, he was afraid and he set his face to seek the Lord.

> *O Lord, God of our fathers, Are you not God in heaven? You rule over all the kingdoms of the nations. In your hand are power and might so that none is able to stand against you* (Chronicles 20:6)

Basically, Jehoshaphat acknowledged he was powerless and did not know what to do. But he also told the Lord that "our eyes are upon You." This chapter is a prophetic picture for a believer established in the Lord today!

When Jehoshaphat set his eyes on the Lord and began proclaiming what he already knew of the greatness and faithfulness of God, He answered mightily.

Thus Says the Lord:

1. You don't have to fight this battle. It's not yours—it's mine.

2. Position yourself (stand firm; hold your position).

3. Stand still.

4. Do not fear or be dismayed.

5. *Believe in the Lord your God,* and you will be established.

Wow! That is our God today! So how do we respond? Jehoshaphat and the people fell down on their faces and worshipped! Then they gave thanks expecting God to do what He said

Pharaoh Has Been Challenged

He would do. Give thanks to the Lord, for His steadfast love endures forever. Then the Lord set an ambush against the enemy! He responded to their praise and thanksgiving before the battle—they believed God and it was evident in their praise!

Jehoshaphat's Prayer:

*After this the Moabites and Ammonites, and with them some of the Meunites, came against Jehoshaphat for battle. Some men came and told Jehoshaphat, "A great multitude is coming against you from Edom, from beyond the sea; and, behold, they are in Hazazon-tamar" (that is, Engedi). Then **Jehoshaphat was afraid and set his face to seek the Lord**, and proclaimed a fast throughout all Judah. And Judah assembled to seek help from the Lord; from all the cities of Judah they came to seek the Lord.*

*And Jehoshaphat stood in the assembly of Judah and Jerusalem, in the house of the Lord, before the new court, and said, **"O Lord, God of our fathers, are you not God in heaven? You rule over all the kingdoms of the nations. In your hand are power and might, so that none is able to withstand you.** Did you not, our God, drive out the inhabitants of this land before your people Israel, and give it forever to the descendants of Abraham your friend? And they have lived in it and have built for you in it a sanctuary for your name, saying, 'If disaster comes upon us, the sword, judgment, or pestilence, or famine, we will stand before this house and before you—for your name is in this house—and cry out to you in our affliction, and you will hear and save.' And now behold, the men of Ammon and Moab and Mount Seir, whom you would not let Israel invade when they came from the land of Egypt, and whom they avoided and did not destroy—behold, they reward us by coming to drive us out of your possession, which you have given us to inherit. **O our God, will you not execute judgment on them? For we are powerless against this great horde that is coming against us. We do not know what to do, but our eyes are on you."***

Meanwhile all Judah stood before the Lord, with their little ones, their wives, and their children. And the Spirit of the Lord came upon

Jahaziel the son of Zechariah, son of Benaiah, son of Jeiel, son of Mattaniah, a Levite of the sons of Asaph, in the midst of the assembly. And he said, "Listen, all Judah and inhabitants of Jerusalem and King Jehoshaphat: Thus says the Lord to you, 'Do not be afraid and do not be dismayed at this great horde, for the battle is not yours but God's. Tomorrow go down against them. Behold, they will come up by the ascent of Ziz. You will find them at the end of the valley, east of the wilderness of Jeruel. You will not need to fight in this battle. Stand firm, hold your position, and see the salvation of the Lord on your behalf, O Judah and Jerusalem.' Do not be afraid and do not be dismayed. Tomorrow go out against them, and the Lord will be with you."

Then Jehoshaphat bowed his head with his face to the ground, and all Judah and the inhabitants of Jerusalem fell down before the Lord, worshiping the Lord. And the Levites, of the Kohathites and the Korahites, stood up to praise the Lord, the God of Israel, with a very loud voice.

*And they rose early in the morning and went out into the wilderness of Tekoa. And when they went out, Jehoshaphat stood and said, "Hear me, Judah and inhabitants of Jerusalem! Believe in the Lord your God, and you will be established; believe his prophets, and you will succeed." And when he had taken counsel with the people, he appointed those who were to sing to the Lord and praise him in holy attire, as they went before the army, and say, "Give thanks to the Lord, for his steadfast love endures forever." And when they began to sing and praise, the Lord set an ambush against the men of Ammon, Moab, and Mount Seir, who had come against Judah, so that they were routed. For the men of Ammon and Moab rose against the inhabitants of Mount Seir, devoting them to destruction, and when they had made an end of the inhabitants of Seir, they all helped to destroy one another. **The Lord delivers Judah.** When Judah came to the watchtower of the wilderness, they looked toward the horde, and behold, there were dead bodies lying on the ground; none had escaped. When Jehoshaphat and his people came to take their spoil, they found among them, in great numbers, goods, clothing, and precious things,* *which they took for themselves until they could carry no more. They were three days in taking the spoil, it was so much. On the fourth day they assembled in the Valley of Beracah, for there they blessed the Lord. Therefore the name of that place has been called the Valley of Beracah to this day. Then they returned, every man of Judah and Jerusalem, and Jehoshaphat at their head,* **returning to Jerusalem with joy, for the Lord had made them rejoice over their enemies.** *They came to Jerusalem with harps and lyres and trumpets, to the house of the Lord.* **And the fear of God came on all the kingdoms of the countries when they heard that the Lord had fought against the enemies of Israel.** *So the realm of Jehoshaphat was quiet, for his God gave him rest all around* (2 Chronicles 20:1-30).

In the world today, people need to hear "thus says the Lord," rather than retreating to empty philosophies and foreign health modalities for our body, soul, and spirit. We are the temple of the Holy Spirit; we belong to God. We were purchased and are no longer our own, but we are bondservants to Christ. He is all we need. He is enough! He has given us everything we need to live life, and He is our Sustainer.

The Lord will perfect that which concerns me; Your mercy, O Lord, endures forever; Do not forsake the works of Your hands (Psalm 138:8 NKJV).

One can easily become overwhelmed with the darkness of the earth, the captivity of Christians, and non-Christians ensnared into the convoluted worldly deception of lies that seem truth to them. We keep our eyes and our hearts set on Jesus. We praise Him and thank Him for what He has done, is doing, and is getting ready to do 'to perfect that which concerns me'. It will be hard to be a Christian in the last days, but just as Jehoshaphat prayed, we pray! We keep our eyes set on Jesus.

Don't settle for less than God's best. He gave His all on the Cross! Jesus—there is no other name! There is no higher reigning King!

References

Bobgan, M. and Bobgan, D. (2012) *Psycho Heresy: The Psychological Seduction of Christianity.* Santa Barbara, CA: East Gate Publications.

Brown, C. (2013). *The Healing Gods: Complementary and Alternative Medicine in Christian America.* New York: Oxford University Press.

Whitaker, R. (2005) *Anatomy of an Epidemic: Psychiatric Drugs and the Astonishing Rise of Mental Illness in America.* Ethical Human Psychology and Psychiatry, Volume 7, Number 1, 2005.

Stewart, D. (2012). *Healing Oils of the Bible.* Marble Hill, MO: Care Publications.

Olmsted, D. and Blaxill, M. (2017). *Denial: How refusing to face the facts about our autism epidemic hurts children, families, and our future.* New York: Skyhorse Publishers.

Bonnke, R. (2017) *Holy Spirit: Are We Flammable or Fireproof?* Orlando, FL: CFAN Publishers.

Heckenlively, K. and Mikovits, J. (2015/2017) *PLAGUE.* New York: Skyhorse Publishers.

Popoola, M. (2015) *Holistic and Complementary Therapies.* Brockton, MA: CE Express Western Schools.

Henley D, Lipson N, Korach K, Bloch C. *Prepubertal Gynecomastia Linked to Lavender and Tea Tree Oils.* New England Journal of Medicine, Feb. 1, 2007.

Eight

God's Redemptive Plan Includes Healing and Provision

What Does God Say? The World Is Still Watching

Hosea gives the historical setting for his ministry in a society much like ours today. Through the outward gauge of that society, people seemed prosperous, enjoyed peace and blessings, yet underneath it all, disaster was imminent. That society had corrupt leaders, unstable families, widespread immorality, class hatred, sickness, and poverty. Though people continued a form of worshipping God, idolatry was more and more acceptable, and the priests were failing to guide the people into God's ways and instructions. Even in the darkness of these days, Hosea proclaims hope to inspire his people to turn back to God. By the way, Hosea, whose name means "salvation" or "deliverance," was chosen by God.

The Book of Hosea teaches how it is important to depend on the presence of the Holy Spirit and that negative things happen when the Holy Spirit is missing from a life. Hosea uses the phrase, "spirit of harlotry" (4:12; 5:4) and tells the consequences of neglecting the Holy Spirit. This spirit of harlotry enslaves the heart, causes people to stray into false ways and false worship, does not witness to Christ, and keeps people from knowing God.

MY people are destroyed for lack of knowledge; because you have rejected knowledge, I reject you from being a priest to me. My people in-

quire of a piece of wood, and then their walking staff gives them oracles. For a spirit of whoredom has led them astray, and they have left their God to play the whore (Hosea 4:6, 12).

In Hosea 7:5-11 we see that because Israel had entered into foreign alliances and assimilated other cultures, it had lost the distinctions that gave it worth. Their alliances, rather than empowering them, have sapped their strength. They became open to deception and easily misled. Israel's foolishness was shown in their thinking that they could find help in any human resource, even powerful Egypt and Assyria.

In Hosea 7:13-16 we see that God wanted to and would have redeemed them, but they rejected His offer. They prayed for provision, although they have removed themselves from a relationship with the Provider.

And in Hosea 8:9 we see that Israel had become dependent on its foreign alliances—hired lovers.

Israel sought to obtain by purchase what God had freely promised: His protection and provision! Wow! Can you see that today? People are paying so much money for health, happiness, and security! God said, "I will be your God." Mercy, forgiveness, grace, and healing are all gifts from a loving God (Psalm 103). But how sad that He is not enough for many! We have been ensnared through unhealthy alliances and are in bondage to other gods to our own destruction.

We have exchanged the glory of God for the opinions of men and things created, rather than desire the Creator (Romans 1). Many can no longer discern what is good and what is God! In our sin of unbelief, many are dying prematurely in torment and pain because we have rejected the God of Abraham to seek after the riches of Egypt and surrounding resources.

Just like with Hosea, God continues to attempt to draw people to Himself. The summary of Hosea is to know God and His ways, to follow Him, to find righteousness, healing, and restoration, and to avoid paths that lead to destruction.

We can recognize that the way we demonstrate God's love through our lives is the most powerful witness of Jesus we will ever offer. People want to know the God of the Bible—they are searching for authenticity! Worship is not just an expression of love like most people think, it is obedience and an expression of love for Him and His ways! When we know Him and follow His ways, we can understand that God's faithfulness is as dependable as the sun that rises every morning. God values our relationship with Him more than He desires our service (Hosea 6).

Pursue and value godly knowledge and wisdom, and see Him as your Healer and Deliverer. The things you don't know can hurt you. Hear the loving heart of the Lord. Though Israel sinned, fell into idolatry, and abandoned God, He still loved His people and could hardly bear to execute the judgment they had brought upon themselves, but there are consequences to disobedience. **"You have eaten the fruit of lies because you trusted in your own way"** (Hosea 10:13). Hosea ends with a plea to return to God:

Oh Ephraim, what have I to do with idols? It is I who answer and look after you; I am like an evergreen cypress; from me comes your fruit. Whoever is wise, let him understand these things; whoever is discerning let him know them; for the ways of the Lord are right, and the upright walk in them, but transgressors stumble in them (Hosea 14:8-9).

Fast Forward

The times of ignorance God overlooked, but now He commands all people, everywhere to repent (Acts 17:30).

Make a fresh commitment to following Jesus. Ask the Holy Spirit to show you areas of unbelief or idolatry in your life. When you think of God's finished work on the Cross through His Son, Jesus, ask God to reveal to you how the fullness of God impacts all of you. What is hindering you from fulfilling what God has called you to do? He desires for you to be all that He has created and redeemed you to be in Jesus' name!

Now this I say and testify in the Lord, that you must no longer walk as the Gentiles do, in the futility of their minds, They are darkened in their understanding, alienated from the life of God because of the ignorance that is in them, due to their hardness of hearts (Ephesians 4:17-18).

Have nothing to do with foolish, ignorant controversies (2 Timothy 2:23).

In the last days, it will be difficult to be a Christian (2 Timothy 3:1 TLB).

He himself bore our sins in his body on the tree, that we might die to sin and live to righteousness. By his wounds you have been healed. For you were straying like sheep, but have now returned to the Shepherd and Overseer of your souls (1 Peter 2:24-25).

2 Peter Chapter 2 describes false prophets and teachers. They are described as 'blaspheming about matters of which they are ignorant and will be destroyed in their destruction.

v. 13 Reveling in their deceptions, while they feast with you…

v. 15 Forsaking the right way, they have gone astray. They have followed the way of Balaam…

v. 19 They promise them freedom, but they themselves are slaves of corruption'.

So that we would not be outwitted by Satan; for we are not ignorant of his designs (2 Corinthians 2:11).

TESTIMONY

A young college student was having problems related to intense anxiety and depression. She had been on psychoactive drugs for several years, and her fear was intensifying. I

God's Redemptive Plan Includes Healing and Provision

prayed with her and asked her to ask the Holy Spirit to reveal a time when she wasn't depressed and what had changed. He took her to a time in her life when she was making bad choices and friendships in order to belong. Then she realized that she had been believing a lie—a need to belong. When she realized she already belonged to the King of Kings, as a child of God, she renounced the lie and asked God to help her embrace the Truth of what He says about her. Immediately, she said she felt loved and the presence of God. Anxiety, fear, and depression dropped off her, in Jesus' name. She is doing better in school, leading small groups, and no longer needing all the drugs.

For God has not given us the spirit of fear; but of power, and of love, and of a sound mind (2 Timothy 1:7).

TESTIMONY

A woman in her 60s had previous suicide attempts, medications for anxiety and continuous suicide ideation. She was fearful of being home alone. She has been attending church for years and was saved, baptized, and filled with the Holy Spirit. When we prayed, I had her repeat after me. When we began to declare 2 Timothy 1:7, she stopped at the words "sound mind" and said, "I don't believe that because I don't have a sound mind." I showed her the Scripture and had her read it. When she realized she was believing a lie—something contrary to what God said—she embraced the reality of truth. She realized that if she received Jesus, she also received a sound mind and not fear and destruction. She asked Jesus for forgiveness, renounced the lie, and declared the truth. She told the tormenting spirit to leave in Jesus' name! She is now laughing—her whole countenance has changed and she no longer takes meds and has no more anxious and suicidal thoughts!

John 6:63 says that *God's words are Spirit and Life!* When the Holy Spirit leads us, we don't just see the natural. The Holy Spirit empowers us to understand what we see in the natural. We can then walk accordingly by the divine principles of the Kingdom of God. We have God's assurance that He will confirm His Word! Begin to renew your mind with His Word.

Salvation Is NOW

God's redemption includes healing and provision. Salvation is not just eternal life after we die. Eternity with Christ begins the day that we invited Jesus in our life to make Him Lord of our life. Salvation is a Person—Jesus Christ! Salvation is all of God impacting all of me. I am rescued, made whole, and complete in Jesus. He is my Savior, my Healer, my Baptizer in the Holy Spirit, and my soon returning King!

We seem to compartmentalize our salvation. Salvation is wholeness—the opposite of compartmentalized. It is easy to speak of salvation as our soul going to heaven one day, but we need to embrace what Jesus preached, "The Kingdom of Heaven is at hand." When we are translated from the kingdom of darkness to His Kingdom of Light because of the Cross of Calvary, everything changed for us *now*, not just in heaven. Jesus is the intersection of heaven invading earth and that impacts me greatly. We are to be a witness of a living, resurrected Christ that has commissioned us to go make disciples, heal the sick, cast out demons, and raise the dead. God confirms His Word with signs and wonders that followed (Mark 16:20; Matthew 10:8; 28:18-20).

The early disciples were described as turning the world upside down. Why? They dared to believe their resurrected Savior. Because of Jesus' death and resurrection, they could know their God! He has not changed—we have! The good news is that He is wooing us back! Those that have ears to hear, let him hear!

He shall seduce with flattery those who violate the covenant, but the

God's Redemptive Plan Includes Healing and Provision

people who know their God shall stand firm and take action (Daniel 11:32). (The NKJV says *do great exploits.*)

The word "know" in Hebrew and Greek both reflect a knowledge—not mind-knowledge, like information, but obtaining knowledge from experience. Most healthcare professionals understand this term, because most of their knowledge came from hands on clinical or laboratory experiences, not just book knowledge.

Testimony

In 2003, I took my first trip to Africa. I had been learning about healing and the full Gospel as it applied today. There were several options available to go with a prayer team for international healing crusades. In my prayer time, I sensed the Lord speaking to me that I was going to Africa, so I signed up for the crusade trip to Africa. As the months went by, I began preparing for the trip. Several weeks out, I acquired a nasty spider bite on my thigh. It was large, red, and painful. I stood in every prayer line and just kept believing for healing. A few weeks before the trip, I was sitting in my closet at home, and I realized that now the bite had a black hardened area in the middle of the bite (necrotic tissue). My nurse mind starting racing about how I could not go to Africa with a draining wound because this type of wound would need to be debrided. Before I could give voice to any of my thoughts, the Holy Spirit interrupted me and reminded me of my prayer time, when God said I was going to Africa.

I stood up and out of my mouth came the words, "Wait, what did God say? Satan, listen up, this is a trick. God said I am going to Africa, so in the name of Jesus, I am healed!" I stomped my foot because I was mad that I had almost been seduced into believing I could not go. That day, I went to work as usual. At that time I was the director of health and wellness at a local university. I was walking the track that afternoon when I realized that my clothes were not irritating the painful wound on my leg. In fact, I had no pain. I went into the dressing room to discover that the bite was still very large, but now it was light pink with no black or infectious center. The next day it was completely gone. The lesson for me that day began my journey to pay attention to what God says and not what I see as an obstacle or contrary to it.

Needless to say, I went to Africa and saw many miracles. I came home with soaring faith and a renewed commitment to not settle for just anything but to pursue Jesus and His Kingdom for my family. I have been catapulted into a lifestyle of healing and deliverance. I am passionate about seeing people saved, healed, set free, and walking in the power of the Holy Spirit.

This is an example of the "knowing" that is acquired by experienced knowledge not information knowledge. What is stopping you from fulfilling your call? What are you accepting or tolerating that is contrary to what God said?

Freedom and Health Is the Presence of Someone

Freedom isn't the absence of something but the presence of Someone!

Mental health philosophies produce bondage; Jesus purchased freedom! Healing and deliverance is simply to identify the oppression and eliminate it. It is the simplicity of the Gospel. Believe the person Jesus for who He is—the Healer (not the healing). His desire is to transform us from the inside out. Many times physical symptoms are an indication of something internal—soul (mind, emotions, or will) or spirit. When this is the case, the physical healing will manifest when the internal healing takes place.

God's Redemptive Plan Includes Healing and Provision

Freedom is the solution—promise focused, not problem focused. The Holy Spirit was the One who was there when a person derailed and is the *only* Person who can restore and heal our innermost soul (will, mind, emotions).

The thing on which we are focused organizes our life. If we are focused on depression, for example, or diabetes, managing depression or diabetes will order all the other things pertaining to our daily lifestyle. We were not created to be managed under a chronic condition, but to be whole, free, and effective witnesses of a resurrected, living, and personable God.

But seek first the Kingdom of God and His righteousness and all these things will be added unto you. 34 Therefore do not be anxious about tomorrow, for tomorrow will be anxious for itself. Sufficient for the day is its own trouble (Matthew 6:33-34).

If we seek God first in everything, He will back up His Word in power and provision to accomplish what He has instructed us to do to accomplish His purposes upon the earth. It is the simplicity of the Gospel.

Because we have reduced the Holy Spirit to "speaking in tongues" or refer to Him as "it," few people value the gift and baptism of the Holy Spirit. The Holy Spirit is a Person who is valuable and essential to knowing God and accomplishing our assignment, as well as increasing our maturity and preparation to be the bride for whom Christ is coming. It is no wonder we lack discernment, empowerment, and stamina.

Romans 1 declares that when we have exchanged the glory of God for the things created, the consequence is that the Lord Himself turns us over to a reprobate mind (no longer discerning; degenerate, outcast, rejected). We need Holy Spirit counsel and empowerment. He is not optional to an authentic Christ follower!

Where there is no prophetic vision the people cast off restraint, but blessed is he who keeps the law (Proverbs 29:18).

Deliverance Is Not Complicated

Deliverance is not Regression therapy! Deliverance is eliminating the oppression of the enemy; and breaking chains that bind me to this world so I can be free to be what God meant for me.

1. Know who you are in Christ.
   - Jesus is the name of absolute authority.
   - Our power source is Jesus (His Spirit) by faith in His Word.

   Faith is the connector—we are healed/saved by grace—a gift to receive!)

2. Recognize the enemy. Stand against him!
3. Don't settle for bondage. Stand firm on what God says!

But God, being rich in mercy, because of the great love with which he loved us, even when we were dead in our trespasses, made us alive together with Christ—by grace you have been **saved** (Ephesians 2:4-5).

For by grace you have been **saved** *through faith…For we are his workmanship, created in Christ Jesus for good works, which God prepared beforehand that we should walk in them* (Ephesians 2:8-10).

Definitions of Saved

- *Strong's* 4982 *sozo* (save, heal, preserve, rescue, into His provision)
- *NASB Exhaustive Concordance* (cured, salvation, made well, recover, restore, ensure)
- *Thayer's Greek Lexicon* (to keep safe and sound, rescue from danger or destruction, restore to health, make well, heal)

Divine healing is the act of God's grace, by the direct power of the Holy Spirit, by which the physical body is delivered from

God's Redemptive Plan Includes Healing and Provision

sickness and disease and restored to soundness of health.

—Marie Woodworth-Etter

Whatever you need—the answer is always the same—Jesus!

I am the vine; you are the branches. Whoever abides in me and I in him, he it is that bears much fruit, for apart from me you can do nothing (John 15:5).

Nine

Calling All Full Gospel Believers

Modern history is filled with individuals who believed in the Full Gospel for healing and deliverance, not only salvation in terms of eternal life after we die: Smith Wigglesworth, Marie Woodworth-Etter, John G. Lake, John Alexander Dowie, Aimee Semple McPherson, David Wilkerson, and Reinhard Bonnke, to name a few.

It is so interesting. I also came across a Canadian medical doctor and surgeon who traded her vocation to become a healing evangelist. Dr. Lilian Yeomans (1861-1942) practiced medicine and surgery for many years in a large city serving the poor, those with addictions to alcohol, and others in other hard places. She also became addicted to stress relievers, especially morphine, to help her sleep. She believed that she was always in control, but the addiction cost her greatly. None of her colleagues could help her. When she was literally bedridden and dying, she read the Bible and discovered healing throughout the Scriptures. She had always prayed, but never believed God healed.

When the truth of God's healing power became a reality, Dr. Yeomans believed God with childlike faith. She was miraculously and totally healed. She became an ordained minister and missionary and traveled to the US and Canada to preach about the healing power of God. She is well published in books and magazines that include the *Pentecostal Evangel*. She opened what were called faith homes. People could choose to come for faith healing instead of medical treatment. In the faith homes, prayer and the Word of God was spoken over people continually and many were healed. What happened to those homes? If anyone reading this would like to partner with me to develop these faith-life homes again, please consider contacting me to do so. I believe this is an example of the Book of Acts for today.

A great history source for you is the Healing and Revival Press: www.healingandrevival.com.

Below is a quote from Dr. Yeomans when she experienced an acute condition.

> I have always been convinced (of course I do not ask anyone to share my views) that I should have lost my life if I had disobeyed the Gentle Voice that told me to go home, away from human skill and the resources of Surgical Science, to the Secret Place of the Most High. This I know, He has never failed and never will fail the heart that trusts Him. *(Digital Copyright 2004 by Healing and Revival Press. Excerpt from 1915 "Triumphs of Faith' magazine. Used with Permission.)*

Treasure the Voice of God

And Samuel said to all the house of Israel, 'If you are returning to the Lord with all your heart, then put away the foreign gods and the Ashtaroth from among you and direct your heart to the Lord and serve him only, and he will deliver you out of the hand of the Philistines'. 4) So the people of Israel put away the Baals and the Ashtaroth, and they served the Lord only (1 Samuel 7:3-4).

For this commandment that I command you today is not too hard for you, neither is it far off…but the word is very near to you. It is in your mouth and in your heart, so that you can do it. "See, I have set before you today life and good, death and evil. If you obey the commandments of the Lord your God that command you today, by loving the Lord your God, by walking in his ways, and by keeping his commandments, and his statures and his rules, then you shall live and multiply and the Lord your God will bless you in the land that you are entering to take possession of it. But if your heart turns away, and you will not hear, but are drawn away to worship other gods and serve them, I declare to you today that you shall surely perish. You shall not live long in the land that you are going over the Jordan to enter and possess. I call heaven and earth to witness against you today, that I have set before you life and death, blessing and curse. Therefore choose life, that you and your offspring may live, loving the Lord your God, obeying his voice and holding fast to him for he is your life and length of days" (Deuteronomy 30:11-20).

If you diligently heed the voice of the Lord your God and do what is right in His sight, give ear to His commandments and keep all His statutes, I will put none of the diseases on you which I have brought on the Egyptians. For I am the Lord who heals you (Exodus 15:26 NKJV).

He went about doing good and healing all who were oppressed by the devil (Act 10:38).

"Oh God…We do not know what to do, but our eyes are on you." Thus says the Lord to you, "Do not be afraid and do not be dismayed at the great horde, for the battle is not yours but God's.' You will not need to fight this battle. Stand firm, hold your position, and see the salvation of the Lord on your behalf" (2 Chronicles 20:12,15,17).

Jesus said to the Jews who believed Him, "If you abide in my word, you are truly my disciples. And you will know the truth and the truth will set you free" (John 8:31-32).

"I am the vine; you are the branches. Whoever abides in me and I in Him, he it is that bears much fruit, for apart from me you can do nothing" (John 15:5).

"The thief comes only to steal and kill and destroy. I come that they might have life and more abundantly" (John 10:10).

Calling All Full Gospel Believers

For Christ did not send me to baptize but to preach the gospel, and not with words of eloquent wisdom lest the cross of Christ is emptied of its power. For the word of the Cross is folly to those perishing, but to us who are being saved, it is the power of God (1 Corinthians 1:17-18).

For I decided to know nothing except Jesus Christ and Him crucified. And my speech and my message were not in plausible words of wisdom, but in demonstration of the Spirit and power so that your faith might not rest in the wisdom of men, but the power of God (1 Corinthians 2:2-5).

For the Kingdom of God does not consist in talk but in power (1 Corinthians 4:20).

The good news is that God has given His Son, Jesus, who gave His life so that we could have life! He died and was resurrected and gives each of us an opportunity to be reconnected to this same God now and forever. All others are perishing, but as people, we choose! Healing is a blessing!

TEN

The Final Hour Is Here: A Prophetic Warning

The first two chapters of Revelations speak about Jesus walking among seven churches that represent our current state of affairs. God is giving a warning to those He loves because the end of the world is near. The world is not falling apart but falling into place! God has an appointed time in which He will say, "Enough!" and judgment will fall on those that did not choose Him. We can see all around us biblical prophecy coming into play as in the last days. No one should be surprised, but this period in time should be a critical time for each believer in Christ to evaluate their relationship with Christ. Pay attention to His Word and His Ways, and be watchful for His soon return.

There were two churches, Smyrna and Philadelphia, with which God was pleased and did not tell them to repent. Two things common to these particular churches that were lacking in the others: *they were steadfast in their faithfulness to trust God* and *they kept His Word.* They were poor by the world's standards but were rich in that they possessed spiritual character and had peace.

Author and Pastor David Ravenhill describes in detail the prophetic warning to the universal church in his book, *For God's Sake, Listen!* He details the book of Revelation in God's prophetic warnings to the seven churches and compares them to the church today. To summarize, the central theme of each are as follows. The Spirit is speaking to the Church as a whole so we can prepare ourselves for persecution in cultural wars that give opportunity to stand up for God's Word and His Truth.

1. EPHESUS—Left their First Love.

Jesus must be first in everything! First love is measured by priority, intensity, quality, and purity. Everything else is worthless. James 4:4—*whoever wishes to be a friend of the world makes himself an enemy of God.* As a bride and bridegroom—the Lord desires a people whose one goal is to bring pleasure to the heart of God.

2. SMYRNA—Spiritually rich church—found to be faithful!

3. PERGAMUM—The compromising church.

Pergamum represents those that decide they can maintain some of kind of Christian credibility and also be linked without separation to the world. Pergamos is a picture of any church or believer that marries paganism in any form. This was a religious center where pagan cults worshipped Athena, Asklepios (or Asclepius), Dionysius (which is another name for Bacchus the god of drunkenness and debauchery), and Zeus (the Greek god of the sky and thunder, the king of all other gods and men). These are real demons, but we call it mythology. God calls Pergamum the place where Satan's throne is. The Greek god Asclepius was a well-known deity all over the ancient world and is associated with healing and medicine. His image is the logo for the World Health Organization and the symbol of the American Medical Association. Interesting that the emblem still embraced today in medicine and healthcare is the god of healing and the ancient guild of doctors.

The symbol is the serpent winding around a pole or Asklepios' rod or staff. Many are worshipping and ensnared to the bronze snake instead of a risen Christ. Satan has people looking to the counterfeit instead of the empty Cross because Jesus is alive and our Healer today.

This city was also noted for its medical school and physicians such as Galen and Hippocrates—called the father of modern medicine. Both contributed to the philosophical foundation of psychology (*psyche*—Greek word for soul).

What is interesting here is that the Lord commends this church for not denying His name and for personal faithfulness to Him. However, He did say they began to tolerate false teachers and subsequently, began to adopt practices of Balaam that led people away to destruction.

Numbers 22-24 tells the story of Balaam. God instructed Balaam two different times not to do something that he knew was probably wrong. The third time, God gave him permission, but only because of Balaam's insistence. It is clear that God was angry with him. Balaam typifies all of us who exalt our own desires and pressure God, all the while rationalizing what it is we want to do to give in to compromise.

We go our own way as opposed to God's way and believe God is okay with it. And how often God permits us to have our way—and we call it God's *permissive will*—but in the end is the way of death. When our way is contrary to God's revealed will, we too are heading in the way of Balaam. The way of Balaam gives place to the error of Balaam (Jude 11). The word "error" used here is the Greek word for delusion, deception, fraudulent, or to wander. Balaam's rationalizing his own way opened him to deception and error.

Paul warns that every one of us is susceptible to wandering from the truth.

> *...because they refused to love the truth (God's way) and so be saved. Therefore God sends them a strong delusion, so that they may believe what is false* [follow an erroneous line of reasoning] (2 Thessalonians 2:10b-11).

Balaam had allowed himself to follow a false line of reasoning. He did so because he wanted what was being offered to him.

Because of this false line of reasoning, he had deceived himself that God was okay with it and wouldn't mind so much if he cursed the people of Israel. He devised a plan to introduce corruption by counselling Israel that God would never curse them, which allowed the Israelites to mingle and marry the daughters of Moab and join in their festivities and celebrations.

The teaching of Balaam corrupted Israel. The people of God violated God's call to separation, and they freely mixed with the heathens, not only worshipping their gods but also conceiving children with them. God saw this blatant display of idolatry and immorality, and he released judgment and over 24,000 men died in a plague.

Basically, the principle Balaam used revolves around the idea that because they were the blessed covenant people of God, they could not be cursed—that they might, with safety and security, indulge themselves in social intercourse with their neighbors for they reasoned that no harm could come to them.

Now these things happened to them as an example, and they were written for our instruction, upon whom the ends of the ages has come. Therefore, let anyone who thinks that he stands take heed lest he fall (1 Corinthians 10:11-12).

Interesting! Balaam began to leave the way of the Lord because he was dazzled by the promise of wealth and the taste of the world's goods. What about today? People promise health, wealth, miracles, and even extended life outside our God!

The body of Christ let themselves be deceived. The deception stemmed from the thinking that their wealth and prosperity was a sign of God's blessings. The deception is that because we believe we are under blessing and not judgment, God is not concerned about how we live or in whom we seek counsel and healing. Let the Holy Spirit speak to you personally about those aspects of your life in which you have been deceived or perhaps perceive that God is not interested in what we seek or do. However, the truth is that

Jesus is interested in being Lord in all areas of your life. Do you believe He is sufficient? You are complete in Him.

God's command is simple, "Repent, turn around, and go another way." Unbelief and going a different way than His revealed will, He calls sin! He said if they did not repent and do something about the compromise and tolerance, He would make war against them with the sword of His mouth (Revelation 2:16).

We can't tolerate idols or evil in any form. First Corinthians 5:6 says a little leaven, leavens the whole lump. There is no room for compromise. Have you considered that your troubles may stem from God at war against the thing you are choosing?

> *The sorrows of those who run after another god multiply; and their drink offerings of blood I will not pour out or take their names on my lips. The Lord is my chosen portion and my cup; you hold my lot* (Psalm 16:4-5).

Another teaching God called out was the teaching of the Nicolaitans, which is now called Antinomian heresy. It is the false belief of eternal security that says we are secure in Jesus' name and our faith, and it matters little about our conduct or actions. Israel's union with the Moabites cost many lives. This judgment showed us the extent of God's intolerance and anger against mixture of any kind!

We talk much about spiritual warfare and coming against Satan and the demonic realm. Yet, in Revelation we see a God that is willing to go to war against His Church if that is what it takes to bring her back to His ways and turn her away from the evil ways, error, and insidious teachings that are destroying her.

4. THYATIRA—the tolerant church

This church had a deep devotion to the Lord, free from self and worldly pleasures, and they maintained their passion and purity. What was wrong? They tolerated Jezebel. This is not a spirit nor was this the same Jezebel that was Ahab's wife. Jezebel here refers to a woman—not a controller or manipulator as we often think. She was a self-appointed and self-anointed prophetess who elevated herself to teacher. She worked in isolation and was not part of the five-fold team. She was highly influential and taught false teaching; therefore, she led many in error because of her influence. It was this influence that got her termed as a controlling spirit. Control and manipulation are never mentioned but immorality and idolatry are. Her problem was that she was leading people away from the truth. God's mercy is always so amazing. He gave her time to repent as He is doing now.

In the modern church we see this happening in our midst and we are tolerating it. We see the fruit of false teaching—immorality and idolatry (sickness, premature death, cancer and suicide epidemics, demonic oppression, and turning over the souls of men to humanism and spiritism). We are living in a day when we are mesmerized by someone who has knowledge of the supernatural or prophetic, especially the satanic realm.

Although allopathic and alternative medicine are now steeped in the supernatural realm, with such things as therapeutic touch, Reiki, hypnosis, life force energy, contemplative meditation, transpersonal psychology, heart-based living, and metaphysics—they are not God. He commends the believers in this church who have not learned the depths of Satan. Be alert to spiritualists who say they are believers but do things like spiritual mapping, identification repentance, reconciliation movements, warfare in high places, or wellness initiatives using Scripture and Christian words, but the blood of Jesus and His finished work on the Cross is not at the center or the emphasis. Jesus is sufficient to pull down strongholds and set us free. When He said it was finished, it was, it is, and it forever will be!

Jesus is perfect theology. He modeled and demonstrated the heart of the Father in every situation. He touched everyone who came to Him. Because of Calvary, Jesus' death, burial, and resurrection, we can settle the issue that salvation, healing, and deliverance are in the atonement. Jesus paid the price. Through His act of love, He became a complete triumph over Satan and the kingdom of darkness.

The atonement affords freedom from every bondage:
- Freedom from bondage of sin.
- Freedom from bondage to guilt and shame.
- Freedom from bondage to demonic oppression, to any or all satanic activity.
- Freedom from bondage to sickness, disease, and mental illness.

We receive salvation (saved, healed, and set free) by His free gift of grace and not works. We believe in Jesus and we believe Jesus—not only in the Person, but we believe Him and take Him at His Word.

> *My son, give attention to my words; incline your ear to my sayings. Do not let them depart from your eyes; keep them in the midst of your heart; for they are life to those who find them, and health to all their flesh. Keep your heart with all diligence, for out of it spring the issues of life* (Proverbs 4:20-23).

The sin for this church was having a tolerance for things they should not have tolerated. We have repackaged God into our own liking. Because all things belong to God, we often rationalize that we don't have to be separate, and nothing is forbidden. We tell people that God understands our weaknesses and our hang-ups because we are afraid of offending people by calling sin what it is! We are afraid to tell people that Jesus is greater than their medicines and the counsel of people with non-biblical viewpoints. Jude tells us to earnestly contend for our faith—*to guard what we have been given and what we have been taught.* By softening our approach to grace, we offend a holy God. We want our pain and discomfort eliminated at any cost or adversity except the Cross. We treat God with a situational relationship rather than a relational lifestyle of trusting Him.

Herein lies the idolatry: This new "user-friendly" god is far more interested in our happiness, health, and prosperity than our holiness. Holy passion for the things of God has been replaced by personal passion, and fulfillment, and immediate elimination of any stress, discomfort, or pain. Instead of speaking peace, we take a pill, engage in the latest promotion of health, or take comfort in another person.

This is what will happen if you turn back and worship the One true God to whom idolatry, unbelief, and immorality really count as sin. Anyone teaching on discipline, holiness, commitment, or obedience is said to have a religious spirit. Now, the Body of Christ tolerates sin, but has little tolerance for talk about being separated from the world and the cost of discipleship.

Let the Scriptures and the Holy Spirit search our minds and hearts (Revelation 2:23). "Hearts" literally means kidneys. The kidneys filter and eliminate toxins. Thyatira was experiencing kidney failure! We need to heed the Spirit's warning. Are we allowing ourselves to be poisoned and toxified by our tolerance of idolatry and immorality? We put toxins into our bodies without hesitation; we are no longer cautious about what is being absorbed in our minds through our eyes and ears, even when we know these things are causing destruction and untoward consequences. We do not know how to govern ourselves. This is what the Holy Spirit must restore if we are to be powerful witnesses on the earth and have authority with the world.

5. SARDIS—the dead church

With all the churches, it is clear that God looks upon the heart—the inside which may not at all reflect what we see on the outside. Revelation 3:1b says, "You have a name that you are alive, but you are dead." Sardis is the only church that did not receive any commendation, but yet it was the one to attend because of its great reputation in the area. Jesus immediately condemned her for her lack of completed deeds. How easily we can become attenders of church, rather than abiders in Christ. How quickly we can become great in natural efforts and not even miss that the Holy Spirit is not leading. We become whole denominations of humanistic enterprises rather than keeping ourselves unspotted from the world. We settle into compromise.

How Jesus must grieve when His beloved Bride defiles herself by ignoring the Holy Spirit's voice and guiding hand in order to follow a successful person or program. Romans 13:14 says, "make no provision for the flesh" and 1 John 2:6b says we are "to walk, even as (Christ) walked." Jesus warned us that in the last days the love of many would wax cold (Matthew 24:12). There is clouded spiritual vision and spiritual wandering due to false teaching and following worldly ways by thinking there are no consequences.

It is imperative that we know the Word of God. Jesus said He is the Bread of Life, Living Water, and the Breath of Life. Many in the Body of Christ are in a state of failure to thrive: anorexic (malnourished from starving); dehydrated (lack of sufficient water to nourish cells and keep the vital organs functioning); and hypoxic (lack of air). All of these physical things lead to certain death without intervention.

Jesus is the Word. In John 6:63-64, Jesus speaks to His disciples,

It is the Spirit who gives life; the flesh profits nothing. The words that I speak to you are spirit, and they are life. But there are some of you who do not believe (NKJV).

More dangerous than all these is the condition of spiritual deadness—when you can no longer sense the promptings of the life-giving Spirit. He who has an ear, let him hear what the Spirit is saying to the churches.

6. PHILADELPHIA—approved by God and kept His Word

The church in Philadelphia used the power of God daily to stand against constant opposition from those who were in a group Jesus referred to as "the synagogue of satan" (Revelation 3:9). They had relied steadfastly on God, minute by minute, enduring countless daily difficulties and apparent persecutions. They kept His Word and did not deny His name. They did nothing in their human strength or follow the teachings and counsel of philosophy. Jesus stated emphatically that a sign of the last days and His soon coming would be that we would be "hated by all nations because of My name" (Matthew 24:9). He went on to warn that this would mark the beginning of a time when many will fall away. Are we prepared? Again, to whom are we listening and from whom do we take counsel? Invite the Holy Spirit to govern every aspect of your life and to prepare you as His Bride.

7. LAODICEA—the apostate church, the Lukewarm bride

This church was rated the worst by the assessment of many commentaries; however, it is important to remember that God was still walking among them. This means that again, His love and mercy are amazing because He is still wooing people to repent and turn back to Him. For us, love and a longing for restoration can be our only response toward this Church. Jesus longs to be invited once again.

Today, we have learned to excel and are considered a healthy church without the abiding presence of God in our midst. One of the saddest comments regarding this Laodicean church is that they believed they "had need of nothing." This reveals the degree of blindness and deception into which these believers had fallen. The major characteristic is her lukewarmness: she is clean, comfortable, and complacent, even accepting sickness and bondage and torment from the enemy as that is their lot in life. We are comfortable that we are in righteousness and can testify of God's goodness, but see our situation on earth as hopeless until heaven. All of the enemy's lies lead to hopelessness. Have we bought into a Christian subculture just like Laodicea that all is good but we have no passion to press on into greater intimacy and knowledge of God? Or do we have no goal to make disciples, teaching people to observe all that Jesus commanded us to do? (Matthew 28:19-20). What are we teaching by our actions? Do people see Jesus in us—preaching the Kingdom of God is near, healing the sick and speaking peace into storms?

The Ephesians and Laodiceans were similar. The Ephesians could be likened unto a woman who falls madly in love and gets married. She has a fruitful, wonderful relationship with her husband, has children, and is happy. However, after years of household responsibility and familiarity, she slowly loses passion for her husband.

The Laodiceans had a different relationship with the Lord. They were like a woman who dates a man but refuses to marry him because she has other priorities she wants to pursue and other men in her life with whom she doesn't want to sever relationships. Instead, she engages in an off-and-on, shallow relationship with him, keeping him on a string but never committing just to him.

God was not their life or love. They knew about Him and could defend their beliefs when challenged, but as long as they perceived their sins were forgiven, everything was fine.

Despite all this, Christ continues knocking at our door, hoping that we will realize there is no substitute for His Presence. Moses refused to settle for the wealth of Canaan but rather pleaded with God for His presence (Exodus 33:13-16). Have we settled for the milk and honey or do we really desire His presence?

Laodicea failed to understand how close she was to being expelled—vomited up! She was blind to her own condition, not realizing she was being given a final chance for full and a complete recovery so remarkable and given to each of the seven churches: the privilege of sitting and reigning with Christ upon His throne. What grace and what mercy!

Do we realize how great we need today to evaluate where we are in our position with Christ? What position does He hold in your life?

Often Christians are trapped because we fail, so we see ourselves as failures, which leads to more failure. We have been deceived into believing what we do determines who we are. However, our identity is in being a child of God through Jesus Christ who is alive. Freedom in Christ should determine what we do and who and what we pursue. Then we are *working out our salvation* (Philippians 2:12), not *working for* our salvation.

In our new identity—our position in Christ as children of God—we are now a new creation (2 Corinthians 5:17). We are no longer a product of our past. We are a product of Christ's finished work on the Cross. The most important belief that we possess is a true knowledge of WHO God is. The second most important belief is who WE are as children of God. We were never designed to function independently from God. He created and redeemed us to be His, fully alive in Christ, and walking in power and love enabled by the Holy Spirit. Christ completes us (Colossians 2:10-13).

The first requirement for recovery is *repentance*. Repentance means to agree with God in His evaluation of my life, regardless of how I or others view myself. It means to turn from my sin and pride, humbly seeking God for His cleansing. It means opening our hearts again, zealously pursuing a relationship with Him, and making Him the focus and center of our lives.

Following this, we need to spend time with Him and begin to trust and obey His Word for our lives. Revelation 3:19b says, "Therefore be zealous and repent." Zealous means to admire, to be enthusiastic for, to strive after, to have warmth of feeling for. Press in to know and love Him!

Summary Warning to the Church Universal Today

These letters in Revelation are a treasure of truth for teaching, reproof, correction and training. David Ravenhill, author of *For God's Sake, Listen! A Prophetic Word to the Church*, presents a remarkable detailed description of each letter, as well as the prophetic interpretation and summary for the universal church today. As Israel's sins were examples for the early Church and us today, so these failures of the early church serve likewise as a warning to the present-day Body of Christ—both corporately and as individuals.

1. Beware of Falling out of Love

The most important message is our call to a divine personal relationship. He alone must be the love of our life. Christ will not tolerate being relegated to anything but first place. Colossians 1:18b says, "Christ must have first place in everything!" Any person, program, philosophy, or passion that replaces Christ is idolatrous in the sight of God.

2. Beware of Replacements

Replacement processes take place gradually over time.

The greatest dangers today are that we focus on blessings, anointing, gifts, authority, and calling instead of spending time on our relationship with the Father. In time, our love for the inheritance—blessings—replaces our love for God. None of these blessings or gifts was ever meant to become a substitute for our relationship with Christ. Salvation, healing, deliverance, and provision are by-products of knowing, loving, and following Jesus, not to be sought after or to replace Him. Let's love, serve, and want Him!

3. Beware of Compromise

Christ will not tolerate any teaching, doctrine, philosophy, or tradition that leads to compromise with regard to His standard of holiness in His Word. Mass culture has dulled our sensitivity to

God's standards of morality and purity to Him and His Word. We have become insensitive to the seriousness of taking God at His Word. One example is that we talk about all our past illnesses, medications, and treatment regimens. We can refer people to good restaurants, doctors, dentists, and even plumbers—but can we refer a great Scripture and speak God's Word into the inquiring person's life?

Where are the testimonies of God's provision? Why don't we refer people to the Great Physician? I believe many put themselves in grave danger because of unbelief and the lack of knowing our God and His Word. We have many casualties of war. Premature deaths and disabilities due to drugs and treatments in the name of wellness abound when all along God has said He would be our God and for us not to forget His benefits.

4. Beware of the Downward Spiral

First comes the failure to acknowledge some aspect of His lordship over our lives. Other priorities and values, and love for the world itself, replaces Him, which leads to everyone doing what is right in their own eyes. God's call to separate ourselves unto Him is denied.

We then fall into the world's pressure towards toleration. To be tolerant is defined: "to recognize and respect the rights, opinions, and practices of others." Finally, we come to "adopt" this tolerance, which dictionaries define as "to take and follow a course of action, to take on or assume, to choose as a standard." From our position in Christ where we were adopted into God's own family, the Church is sliding downward toward adopting the world and its ways.

Today, the call to come out from among them and be a peculiar and distinct people is met with stiff resistance from God's people because we desire to be popular and trendy. We don't have to be in politics to change or influence a society, we just have to be in love with Jesus and be a separate and peculiar people. Instead, our whole lives have absorbed the world's influence, with its philosophies, practice, and policies. At the bottom of the spiral, we find ourselves adopting the ways of the world, loving our lives so much that we can no longer think about laying them down.

Could it be we have replaced God's Word and standard for health and well-being with the world's modern practices and opinions of man to our own destruction? Have we settled into compromise and accommodation to a culture of scientific inquiry and experiments when no one really understands our health like the Creator? From the beginning, God has said, "I will be your God!"

The people in the New Testament recognized those that turned the world upside down. They would recognize us today if we were faithful and kept God's Word. His power and glory would be demonstrated through our lives as normal, everyday lifestyle of the extraordinary, because we are totally dependent and abiding in Him.

5. Final Warning—Beware Lest Your Light Go Out
As the Book of Revelation began, Christ, through His Spirit, walked among the seven lamps of the seven churches, trimming the wicks and refilling them with oil lest their lights go out, rendering these churches useless and plunging the world in spiritual darkness.

Today the world takes little notice of us except to point out our gross compromises and failures and sometimes the weirdness of our subculture. We fail to present them with a radically different choice, because we have desired to be just like them. We bow to their practices, wisdom, and counsel, and trust in their experts for policies, parenting, miracles and cures for mental bondage and physical disease. Yes, Jezebel and Balaam and the Egyptian, Greek, and Roman gods are alive and well and flourishing among us.

The world sees no differences in worship, entertainment,

health, and well-being in the body of Christ than in the rest of society. However, people are noticing, that in a world with heightened fear and anxiety, the people who talk about the Bible and a supernatural God, act like they really don't believe what they proclaim. Believers and non-believers alike are grasping at anything and anyone that stands out as offering them hope and wellness. This is the same dichotomy in which I noticed several years ago that led me to transition out of healthcare to become a first century Christ follower and to promote spiritual health, God's way! People are watching! People are watching those of us that stand out to proclaim Jesus is Savior, Healer, Deliverer, and Life. Jesus should stand out! Today—the Spirit is calling us once again to come out from their midst and be separate (2 Corinthians 6:17a).

It's Time the Church Heard about Jesus!

The true key to following Christ is faithfulness and obedience to His Word and His ways. It is knowing what God says and paying attention to the leading of the Holy Spirit, not just taking someone else's word or methods. One of the greatest needs of the Church is that we return to the simplicity of God's Word.

It's time the church heard about Jesus again. We have spent far too long pursing other sources of life, health and wellness and need to return to Christ Himself. The Lord longs for His Bride to become healthy and fruitful, to be delivered of her soul-sicknesses and delighted in Him again. It's time for us to return to our first love, the Great Physician, our Healer, our Deliverer, our soon returning King! He has come so that we might have LIFE in all its abundance. He alone has the answers to all our needs. Let's seek Him pressing through all obstacles until we touch Him!

Set Your Eyes on Jesus
We can easily turn aside if our eyes are not fixed on Jesus. Jeremiah said,

> *My people have committed two evils: they have forsaken Me, the fountain (source) of living waters, to hew for themselves cisterns, broken cisterns that can hold no water* (Jeremiah 2:13).

These broken cisterns can be anything we substitute in place of Christ Himself: ministry gifts, congregations, reputations, pride, or people in whom we seek counsel for health and wellness. God is not a means to the end—He *is* the end!

Paul counted all else but Christ as rubbish (Philippians 3:8). Like the woman who touched the hem of Jesus' garment, we need to reach out and take hold of the *only* source of Life—Christ Himself. She suffered many years, had gone to many doctors, and exhausted all her resources, now she was desperate. Jesus and He alone is the answer to all our needs and desires. We can no longer afford to let the ways of the world infect us! Let's respond to His invitation, "If any man thirsts, let him come unto Me, and drink" (John 7:37b).

> *"Behold the days are coming," declares the Lord God, "when I will send a famine on the land, not a famine for bread or a thirst for water, but rather for hearing the words of the Lord"* (Amos 8:11).

Our greatest need today is to not rely on the opinions of men but to hear the Word of the Lord. For too long, believers have adopted the practices of the world and inevitably find that they've strayed into spiritual barrenness and dark places of spiritual adultery with the world, which leads to sickness, despair, and destruction.

Jesus has never left us on our own without a clear path on which to follow Him in an eternal, brand new life that He offers us. Jesus has given us His inherent authority and power to represent Him well as be ambassadors of heaven. It is we who have gone astray and turned to our own ways. The book of Revelation reveals God's desires, the rewards of His presence, and what God hates, which will bring punishment in His absence.

It is dangerous for a person who confesses to be a Christ follower to live according to the descriptions of the other five churches that were given warnings. The Word of God being given to these churches tells us that God is revealing His heart and mind to His People—His Church. We must pay attention, for it is God's timeless instruction to His people, the standards by which we will be measured. Will we be found faithful walking in the ways of God or be found wandering in our own way, seeking success and solutions in our own eyes and by the world's standards? Will we be walking in the perfect will of God or find ourselves in His permissive will (the error of Balaam) that leads to destruction?

The Good News!

The good news is that God gave the seven churches opportunity to repent, and He is giving you time to repent. No one knows the date or hour when Jesus will appear, but He will be coming soon. In Romans 1, Paul tells us that there is absolutely no excuse for any human being not to know God.

> *For although they knew God, they did not honor as God or give thanks to him, but they became futile in their thinking, and their foolish heart were darkened. Claiming to be wise, they became fools. Exchanged the glory of the immortal God for images resembling mortal man and birds and animals and creeping things* (Romans 1:21-23).

Are you among the ones that have fallen away and exchanged the truth about God for a lie and worshipped and served the creature rather than the Creator, who is blessed forever (v. 25)? Romans 1:28 says, "And since they did not see fit to acknowledge God, God gave them up to a reprobate mind." This means you can no longer discern God from evil and will be destroyed.

> *Though they know God's righteous decree that those who practice such things deserve to die, they not only do them but give approval to those who practice them* (Romans 1:32).

God help us with our unbelief, our blindness and deafness in our nation and among those that call on Your name. God demands that we obey Him, deny ourselves, take up our Cross, and follow Him. We are not to walk in darkness but to be separate and distinct from the ways and practices of the world. He demands that we have no other gods before Him, make no graven images, nor bow down to any images or replacements of the true and holy God.

Jesus is the only way, truth, and Life!

Some trust in chariots and some in horses, but we trust in the name of the Lord our God. They collapse and fall, but we rise and stand upright (Psalms 20:7-8).

He who has clean hands and a pure heart, who does not lift up his soul to what is false and does not swear deceitfully. He will receive blessing from the Lord and righteousness from the God of his salvation (Psalm 24:4-5).

All the paths of the Lord are steadfast love and faithfulness, for those who keep his covenant and his testimonies (Psalm 25:10).

Hear, O my people, while I admonish you! O Israel, if you would but listen to me! There shall be no strange god among you; you shall not bow down to a foreign god. I am the Lord your God, who brought up out of the land of Egypt. Open your mouth wide, and I will fill it. But my people did not listen to my voice; Israel would not submit to me. So I gave them over to their stubborn hearts, to follow their own counsels (Psalm 81:8-12).

For the Lord God is a sun and shield; the Lord bestows favor and honor. No good thing does he withhold from those who walk uprightly. O Lord of host, blessed is the one who trusts in you! (Psalm 84:11-12)

Because he holds fast to me in love, I will deliver him; I will protect him, because he knows my name. When he calls to me, I will answer him; I will be with him in trouble; I will rescue him and honor him. With long life I will satisfy him and show him my salvation (Psalm 91:14-16).

The Final Hour Is Here: A Prophetic Warning

For all the gods of the peoples are worthless idols, but the Lord made the heavens (Psalm 96:5).

I will not set before my eyes anything that is worthless. I hate the work of those who fall away; it shall not cling to me. A perverse heart shall be far from me; I will know nothing of evil (Psalm 101:3-4).

Bless the Lord, O my soul, and forget not all his benefits, who forgives all your iniquity, who heals all your diseases, who redeems your life from the pit, who crowns you with steadfast love and mercy, who satisfies you with good so that your youth is renewed like the eagle. the Lord works righteousness and justice for all who are oppressed. He made known his ways to Moses, his acts to the people of Israel. The Lord is merciful and gracious, slow to anger and abounding in steadfast love (Psalm 103:2-8).

It Is Finished!

Whom are you following? It is imperative that we each *know* God. Take heed to what God says in His Word. Jesus is the only way, the truth, and the life. No man comes to the Father (God of Abraham—the Creator of the world) except through Jesus!

Whom are you following? Much confusion regarding Christianity prevails in the world today. Everywhere you turn, books, TV shows, sermons on-line, ministries for healing and deliverance, all use Scripture and even perform miracles. Beware of spiritual leaders—you don't know what people really believe. Actions or fruit demonstrate what a person believes—not words. Everything must line up to the Word of God—God's standard!

Hear God—Read His Word—Believe His Word

Listen to the Holy Spirit to teach and counsel you. Jesus is the Word! God insists that He has a personal relationship with each of us. We are each going to be held accountable for His standard—His Word and His ways. He is the Word of Life (1 John 1:1-3), and He invites us to be one with Him as He is with our Father.

We have assumed that vision and guidance always come from the senior leader. Oh but not true. I believe God is raising up individuals who, like Samuel, are responding to the voice of the Lord, with "Here I am, Lord, your servant is listening." It is interesting that God spoke to Samuel—he was not the priest. The priest was not taking care of the temple in which he had been assigned. Could that be happening today? People rely only on the senior leader without the five-fold ministry gifts. We have people attending churches who are not always in line with its headship, each doing what they want to do. We are so enamored with formulas replicating what seems to be the best practices yet ignoring the voice of the Lord and His ways. Why is the church powerless? Why are we ineffective as authentic witnesses of Jesus Christ?

The world needs to hear and see that no matter what you need, the answer is always the same—Jesus!

My faith is in Him for Life! My faith is not in the miracle or in another person for a situation. My trust is in God—a relational now and a forever life! Every miracle proclaims that Jesus is alive—my trust is in Him.

> *Every word of God proves true; he is a shield to those who take refuge in him* [AMP: true, tested, and refined like silver]. *Do not add to his words, lest he rebuke you and you be found a liar* (Proverbs 30:5-6).

> *The sorrows of those who run after another god shall multiply; and drink offerings of blood that I will not pour out or take their names on my lips. The Lord is my chosen portion and my cup; you hold my lot. The lines have fallen in pleasant places, indeed, I have a beautiful inheritance* (Psalm 16:4-6).

Everything goes back to a good and gracious and amazing Father who allows us to be and do things that are humanly impossible. Even my faith is a gift!

Everything in us and to us is because of His grace. Even healing is not about us, it is *for* us. God is for us not against us. I choose to love, serve, and follow the God of Abraham, Isaac, Jacob, David, and those many others that we find in the Bible, like Paul, that were authentic, radical, followers of Jesus—my God! His grace is all sufficient for me.

The gospel has been compromised, and we are paying the price. Christians no longer believe in the wrath of God anymore. We hear the phrase, "It doesn't matter what you've done—God is not mad at you." That's a lie! We grieve Him with our unbelief and idolatry. He is serious about His Word! He is serious about our trusting and obeying His Word and His ways. He is serious about a personal relationship with us. He is serious about me!

Jesus gave His life so that I could live. He is stretching out His hand to rescue all, but those that don't want Him are perishing. The world has offered replicas and counterfeits for life, health, and well-being. Christians are so entangled with the world's ways and traditions that God's ways are called legalistic, old fashioned, or even mythology. God describes this behavior as spiritual adultery. Ezekiel 16:26 says the Israelites "played the whore with your Egyptian neighbors."

Turn Your Eyes from the Serpent and Look at Jesus!

The world offers up a brass serpent—the caduceus or Asklepios' rod that we have talked about before—to memorialize the brass serpent that Moses symbolized for healing. The world keeps Christians today focused on the brass serpent so that the Cross is not at the forefront any longer.

The brass serpent Moses used was replaced by the Son of God, Jesus Himself, whose death, burial, and resurrection was penalty for my sin. Because of Jesus, I am rescued, restored to our Father, and can partake of His divine nature. When Jesus said it was finished, 'the devil-serpent and his cohorts were forever defeated. Why would we want to go back to Egypt and their gods, traditions, and philosophies, when God said, "Have no one but Me?"

Jesus is alive and living in me! There are so many people being deceived into thinking they are saved. Natural theories have replaced religious explanations. Spiritual traditions and worldviews (based on Egyptian, Roman, Greek, and other foreign traditions) have replaced biblical instruction and doctrine.

Throughout history one can see that men have reduced the immortal soul to consciousness and thought. Others argue that the whole universe can be explained in physical laws—some even admitted their knowledge came from spiritual experiences. It is easy to see why in the 1600s the church leaders held the position that secular methods of cure and practices must have come from God. And then we see more confusion in the Age of Enlightenment when traditional religious values and beliefs are challenged. Reason is viewed as the essence of human nature and science as a way to explain the universe with no further need of God.

Even now, we disregard or are ignorant about the spiritual realm of which God warns us. We are teaching our children to be entertained by darkness such as mythology, as though God is really okay with that. Did it occur to you that the very mythological movies and figures and superheroes that you invite into your homes are the same very real demons that were worshipped and made people do evil in that period of time?

They are the same demons in the world today—just repackaged so that we love them (in contrast to what God said—do not have fellowship with darkness or have no other gods before me). We wonder why kids are tormented and we have so many man-made labels for mental illness. It is because we entertain and give legal right for spiritual darkness to rule in our homes and lives. What do we invite into our own living rooms? Unfortunately, people that believe this way are considered crazy or spiritual fanatics. What does God say—that is what matters.

Ask the Holy Spirit to identify areas in which you have rejected, diluted, or were ignorant of God's Word. Ask the Lord to show you areas of unbelief. Ask Him to let you know in whom are you trusting and serving. Where are your allegiances and to whom and what are you really yoked when it comes to challenges that require faith?

The charge to all those who call themselves Christ followers is to get serious and evaluate who Jesus means to you. Is He really your way, your truth, and your life? Ask the Lord what would is hindering you from being that first century disciple that we read about in the New Testament.

John 15 says that *He is the vine and we are the branches.* Is He really the source of your knowledge, wisdom, values, and beliefs? Every day decisions and actions speak loudly and reflect largely what one believes. Don't be deceived—let the Word of God be the standard in which you evaluate those decisions and beliefs in which you navigate life. Is Jesus really the source and priority of your life?

The Final Hour Is Here

Time is running out—the world is crying in desperation for hope in their world perceived as hopeless; for solutions when they are paying dearly for the temporary counterfeit; for life when all they perceive, even in the body of Christ, are sickness, drugs, and despair. Suicide and prescription drug addiction are now considered epidemics. All lies lead to hopelessness. We can restore hope! Hope is a person—Hope is Jesus!

God's desire is to see people saved, healed, set free, and walking in the fullness of God and their calling as He created and redeemed them to be. Can we trust and allow Jesus to be proclaimed and demonstrated as those disciples that turned the world upside down? Let God's Word be the Source of Life! Jesus set the standard. We have no right to change it or bring it down to a level of our unbelief, experiences, and perceived interpretations as disciples. Jesus desires to enter your situation and turn things around for His glory and to give you Life.

Psalm 106 depicts a thanksgiving psalm and recounts the steadfast love of God for His people from the time He led them out of Egypt. Psalm 106:7-8,13 says,

Our fathers, when they were in Egypt, did not consider your wondrous works; they did not remember the abundance of your steadfast love, but rebelled at the Red Sea. Yet He saved them for His Name's sake, that he might make known His mighty power. But they soon forgot His works; they did not wait for His counsel.

It goes on to describe that they had wants and cravings in the wilderness. They put God to the test in the desert. They had troubles when they began exchanging the glory of God for a graven image and then the idols of other nations.

But they mixed with the nations and learned to do as they did. They served their idols, which became a snare to them. They sacrificed their sons and their daughters to the demons; they poured out innocent blood, the blood of their sons and daughters whom they sacrificed to the idols of Canaan.

Their enemies oppressed them, and they were brought into subjection under their power, many times He delivered them, but they were rebellious in their purposes and were brought low through their iniquity (which is unbelief). Nevertheless He looked upon their distress, when He heard their cry. For their sake He remembered His covenant and relented according to His steadfast love.

Save us O Lord our God—gather us from among the nations (Psalm 106:35-38, 42-45, 47).

They cried to the Lord in their trouble, and he delivered them from their distress. He sent out his word and healed them and delivered them from their destruction. Let them thank the Lord for His steadfast love, for his wondrous works to the children of man! (Psalm 107:19-21).

The Final Hour Is Here: A Prophetic Warning

Whoever is wise, let him attend to these things; let them consider the steadfast love of the Lord (Psalm 107:43).

And we continue to thank God today for His marvelous steadfast love! God sent His only begotten Son, Jesus, to die for our sins. He paid the penalty once for all mankind. God loves you, and He loves me. When Jesus said it was finished and He died, was buried, and was resurrected for you and for me, we were offered life! The day that I made Jesus my Lord, laid down my life, and committed to live His ways, my eternal destiny changed!

We have to choose Him and His ways! He is our only Hope, our Healer, our Deliver, our Provider! If God had any other way for us to be free, cured, provided for, and our eternal destiny changed, He would have told us so. He certainly wouldn't have given His Son over to death if there was another way. He told us that Jesus is the only way! I believe Him for this temporary life on earth as well as all eternity. And as Bible prophecy falls into place, we must look up because King Jesus is coming back for those that are His. Be alert—be sober—be watchful—be encouraged—our Redeemer draweth nigh! *No matter what the question or the issue—the answer is always the same—Jesus!* Live loved!

Now may the God of peace who brought again from the dead our Lord Jesus, the great shepherd of the sheep by the blood of the eternal covenant, equip you with everything good that you may do His will, working in us that which is pleasing in His sight, through Jesus Christ, to whom be glory forever and ever. Amen (Hebrews 13:20-21).

And we know that the Son of God has come and has given us understanding so that we may know him who is true; and we are in him who is true, in his Son Jesus Christ. He is the true God and eternal life. Little children, keep yourselves from idols (1 John 5:20-21).

Beloved, I pray that it may go well with you and that you may be in good health, as it goes well with your soul. For I rejoiced greatly when the brothers' came and testified to your truth, as indeed you are walking in the truth. I have no greater joy than to hear that my children are walking in the truth (3 John 2-4).

Let's praise and worship God. As you pray, tell the enemy that you won't back down and that you will stand strong because Jesus, the greater One, lives in you!

Eleven

Inspecting Your Foundation

*When many of the Jews realized that Jesus was the Messiah, they cried out, "Brothers, what must we do?" Peter said, "Each of you must **repent** of your sins and turn to God, and be **baptized in the name of Jesus Christ** for the forgiveness of your sins. Then you will receive the **gift of the Holy Spirit**"* (Acts 2:37-38).

Following Jesus: Back to the Basics
1. Repent and Turn to God
2. Baptism in Water
3. Baptism in the Holy Spirit

Foundational Truth #1
Repent and turn to God—You must be born again!
"In the Beginning"

In the Book of Genesis, God created man in His own image—male and female. Mankind enjoyed the image of God, the intimacy of God, and unbroken fellowship with God (relationship).

Because God desired true fellowship with man, and not merely a robot to serve Him, He created man with a free will—the right to choose a relationship with God or not. In the Garden of Eden man had many good choices from which to eat and only one choice that represented disobedience. When Adam and Eve disobeyed because they were enticed with what seemed "good" but wasn't what God said, and their rejection of God opened the door for their separation from God. When man chose something other than what God had given him, he basically decided to take his life into his own hands. Instead of living from the wisdom, righteousness, and resources of God, he would now be limited by his knowledge and efforts, ultimately choosing death—a spiritual separation from God. Through this choice, choosing his way over God's way, sin entered the world. When sin entered the world, so did sickness, depression, and despair.

With that tragic decision, man lost his intimacy and his fellowship with the Lord, His Creator, but God's restoration work began immediately. God already had a plan that would allow us back to a right relationship with Him. That first sacrifice—God's providing clothing from animals—pointed toward the ultimate sacrificial Lamb of God—Jesus Himself.

Man's Plunge

After being dismissed from the Garden and barred from the Tree of Life that stood in its midst, Adam begot children that were born after his own kind—sin natured—who were self-centered, disobedient, and rebellious. Everyone born after Adam was born separated from God—spiritually dead—and called a sinner because now man has a sin nature.

For all have sinned and fall short of the glory of God (Romans 3:23 NKJV).

Restoration

And Jesus said, "I have come that they may have life and that they may have it more abundantly" (John 10:10), but no words exceed the splendor or completeness of David's when he said of the Lord, "He restores my soul" (Psalm 23:3). Restoration means the replacing of spiritual death with spiritual life.

Inspecting Your Foundation

The thief does not come except to steal, and to kill and to destroy. I have come that they may have life, and that they may have it more abundantly (John 10:10).

He restores my soul; He leads me in the paths of righteousness for His name's sake (Psalm 23:3 NKJV).

In the Old Covenant, God made a way to temporarily atone for the sin of man through the shedding of the blood of certain animals in the tabernacle by priests. Without this, man would have been completely separated from God. In the New Covenant, through Jesus' sacrifice, man's access to redemption was made clear and permanent.

But when Christ appeared as a high priest of the good things to come, He entered through the greater and more perfect tabernacle, not made with hands, that is to say, not of this creation; and not through the blood of goats and calves, but through His own blood, He entered the holy place once for all, having obtained eternal redemption (Hebrews 9:11-12 NASB).

And according to the Law, one may almost say, all things are cleansed with blood, and without shedding of blood there is no forgiveness (Hebrews 9:22).

Someone had to pay with blood for the price of our sin. We can die in our sin—eternal separation from God. Or we can receive Christ's gift to us—salvation—payment for that sin and the gift of eternal life with Him. Healing, deliverance, restoration are components of the free gift of God's grace for today.

For the wages of sin is death, but the free gift of God is eternal life in Christ Jesus our Lord (Romans 6:23).

We need to be restored back to the Father. For that restoration to take place, we needed an intervention or someone (a Savior) to rescue us. God sent His Son, Jesus, to pay the death penalty, the price for our sin. As one man (Adam) sinned and all of mankind was separated from God, one man (Jesus) died and shed His blood so that all mankind have an opportunity to be restored to God. His plan for redemption was God's love, mercy, grace, and forgiveness of our sins. Oh what a Savior!

We are no longer called sinners, but saints. God's grace empowers us to overcome sin and live through Him because as He is in this world, so are we.

Love has been perfected among us in this: that we may have boldness in the day of judgement; because as He is, so are we in this world (1 John 4:17 NKJV).

How Do We Become Born Again?

REPENT

First, we have to recognize our need for forgiveness, that we are sinners in need of a Savior. We choose to surrender ourselves to Jesus. We once lived for our own desires, but now we are choosing to live according to God's Word and His ways, not our own. This is repentance—a change in direction, attitude, thoughts, and actions. We no longer belong to our desires—we are owned and belong totally to Christ.

MAKE JESUS LORD OF YOUR LIFE

There is no one good but God (Mark 10:18). We are born with a sin nature. That is who we are. We are born separated from God because of Adam's sin. It is not about being good or bad; it is about being fully devoted to following the instructions of Jesus. It is trusting in God and following God's ways—not our own. Our actions or behavior flow from our nature.

The good news is the saving grace of Jesus Christ! His blood paid the price for you to be redeemed, cleaned, and made new. However, this means that no matter how good you think you are, apart from Christ, you are lost for all eternity which means hell (fire and torment). Your good deeds won't save you. Only Jesus' sacrifice on the Cross (His death) can offer you salvation. If you have repented, besides acknowledging, confessing, and believing Jesus as the Son of God, you need to ask Him to forgive you of your sins. *Then make a commitment to follow His ways and make Him Lord over every aspect of your life.*

A change of lifestyle that reflects your new nature (Jesus) will become evident in your life. You will know that you have entered into or have been transferred into the Kingdom of God. This is not the end but just the beginning of your salvation and sanctification process to become all that God created and redeemed you to be. God gave you free will, just like Adam in the garden. You can choose Him and reap the benefits of that relationship, or reject Him and reap the fruit of eternity without Him. The first step in being in a right relationship with God is repentance.

It is the goodness of God that leads us to repentance. (Romans 2:4). It is because of His goodness that we are able to repent and come back to a right relationship with Him.

1. *Repentance is a change in the direction and course of our lives.* By making Jesus our Lord, we change direction because our focus and values changed. We are no longer preoccupied with the same interests, but our eyes are now on knowing God and His plans. By renewing our minds through the Word of God, He will do the change in us. We will see Him transform the way we act, the way we treat people, and the decisions we make as we diligently commit to walk in obedience to Him. It is a full turnaround—people around you will notice! Born-again people no longer have a desire for the things of the world that entice us to sin or to not please God.

2. *Repentance should be a defining moment in our life.* It is not just about saying a prayer, hoping to stay out of hell. It is a sincere prayer of surrendering our life to God. A born-again experience is a defining moment, one you will not forget!

3. *Repentance is not a religion;* it is the beginning of a relationship with a living God.

4. *Repentance is not just a decision*—it is to be resolute to change your alignment of belief and commitment from the Kingdom of Darkness to the Kingdom of Light in Christ Jesus. We will always be citizens of a kingdom. We have a free will to choose in which Kingdom we will belong. We choose whom we will serve and who we allow to rules over us.

Choose for yourselves this day whom you will serve (Joshua 24:15 NKJV).

Therefore, submit to God. Resist the devil and he will flee from you. Draw near to God and He will draw near to you. Cleanse your hands, you sinners, and purify your hearts, you double-minded (James 4:7-8 NKJV).

Whoever has been born of God does not sin, for His seed remains in him; and he cannot sin, because he has been born of God. In this the children of God and the children of the devil are manifest; Whoever does not practice righteousness is not of God, nor is he who does not love his brother (1 John 3:9-10 NKJV).

Jesus answered and said to him, "Most assuredly, I say to you, unless one is born again, he cannot see the Kingdom of God" (John 3:3 (NKJV).

The term "born again" refers to a new beginning with God—becoming reconciled back to God as if we had never let sin separate us from Him. We are a new creature. We no longer have a clean slate in life—we have a new life to live! That is amazing grace!

MAKE JESUS LORD OF YOUR LIFE

Why should we profess Jesus as not only Savior but Lord? In the West, we emphasize the work Jesus did for us as Savior rather than His position as Lord. Lack of submission to His position of authority creates a significant flaw/fault in our foundation.

Inspecting Your Foundation

*As you therefore have received Christ Jesus the **Lord**, so walk in Him, rooted and built up in Him and established in the faith, as you have been taught* (Colossians 2:6-7 NKJV).

We submit to Him as our supreme and only King and then we benefit from His salvation. This plays out:

- Whether or not we see the reason, we firmly adhere to His words, wisdom, counsel, correction, and instruction.
- We no longer evaluate what is good or evil by our perspective. We evaluate by is it God, even if it is good. (The tree of good and evil—both lead to destruction). God is Life.
- We live in Him; His life becomes ours.
- He will not come into our lives as second to anything or anyone else.
- Separating from His Lordship can result in unanswered prayer (disobedience, unforgiveness, not treating people well, etc.).
- It is impossible to follow Jesus without denying our self (forsaking our ways) and embracing His supreme authority. Take up our cross (incorporating empowerment to walk away from sin and the world's systems).
- We can't demonstrate reasoning to truly follow His leadership. I am no longer independent – it is no longer me. Now we can take up the cross and be empowered to live like Christ. We draw from Him.
- The life we have now is by faith in His ability working in and through us.
- It is impossible to love people apart from Christ in us and the demonstration of His love and power through us.
- It is impossible to resist (fight, stand against) the enemy without submitting to the Lordship of Jesus.

In Matthew 7:21 Jesus warns us that today, after His departure, another gospel would be proclaimed and widely accepted that would offer salvation apart from lordship. Examples today are:
- People reduce the Lord to merely a title rather than a position that Jesus holds in their life.
- People will call Him Lord, but not deny themselves, take up their cross and follow Him.

The foundation is vital! Your life must be founded on the Lordship of Jesus Christ.

Foundational Truth #2 - Baptism in Water

Water baptism was important to Jesus. After He rose from the dead, Jesus told His disciples to take the news of His kingdom and His great salvation to the ends of the earth, telling them,

> *Go therefore and make disciples of all nations, baptizing them in the name of the Father and of the Son and of the Holy Spirit, teaching them to observe all things that I have commanded you; and lo, I am with you always, even to the end of the age. Amen* (Matthew 28:19-20).

We are mandated to make disciples of those that choose a relationship with Jesus. That means instructing them in the Full Gospel and the subsequent responses God requires in obedience to be able to mature and walk in the fullness of Him.

What Is Baptism in Water?

Baptism is the first thing Jesus tells us to do in the Great Commission in Matthew 28:19-21. It is widely misunderstood. Baptism is a transition from one kingdom to another.

Baptism is a transition from one kingdom into another. You are buried with Christ and raised to a new life where you now belong to Christ. Baptism is so important that you cannot find a single place in the Bible where someone starts to believe and does not get baptized immediately. (Examples: prison guard and family in the middle of the night—Acts 16; the 3,000 who believed at the same time after Peter preached—Acts 2; the Ethiopian Eunuch—Acts 8) After the cross, everyone who believed was baptized *immediately*.

Water baptism is a very important part of becoming a disciple. You get baptized to belong to Jesus, renouncing yourself as belonging to someone else. (Remember, there are two kingdoms—light/Jesus or darkness/devil). We associate *freedom* with Jesus, not bondage.

Water baptism indicates the seriousness of our commitment to Jesus Christ. It is an act of obedience to our newfound Savior and Lord. It is a visible sign of our spiritual commitment to lay down our life and step into His. People can be healed, set-free, and filled with the Holy Spirit during this one act of obedience. Jesus will meet you in the water!

Therefore we were buried with Him by baptism into death, in order that just as Christ was raised from the dead by the glory of the Father, so we to may walk in a new way of life (Romans 6:4 HCSB).

So you too consider yourselves dead to sin but alive to God in Christ Jesus (Romans 6:11 HCSB).

If we are baptized into Christ Jesus we are baptized into His death (Roman 6:3).

How do we bury sin or bury the old self? We die to it—in baptism. We bury the old man and are raised new in Christ. It is critical to respond in obedience to Christ in Baptism after repentance and committing to follow Jesus as your Savior and Lord.

When people really understand baptism, people can walk in freedom knowing they have died to the sin nature and can be led by the Spirit rather than the flesh. Jesus got baptized, and the Father and the Holy Spirit were present. He was showing us a picture of the fullness of the Godhead (Father, Son, and Holy Spirit Colossians 1:15-23) when the heavens were opened. We too can walk in the fullness of the Godhead when we are submissive to the Lordship of Jesus Christ.

Those who belong to Christ have crucified the flesh and with its passions and desires (Galatians 5:24).

Baptism is not a work for salvation, but a result of obedience after receiving the gift of salvation that allows for the *working of God* in your spirit life. It is a foundational step to freedom, healing, and victory empowered by God's grace.

In our ministry, we have observed people come out of the water healed, set free, and speaking in tongues. One young lady described chains falling off of her neck. She was no longer depressed. In fact, she came out of the water laughing and speaking in tongues. Her mom told us that she had not laughed in many months. There is no reason to wait to receive the baptism in the Holy Spirit!

Foundational Truth #3—Baptism in the Holy Spirit

It is important for us to live as disciples/followers of Christ. Just as with water baptism, there is a clear pattern in the book of Acts demonstrating that it was expected or normal for every disciple of Christ to be baptized with the Holy Spirit. The Holy Spirit is available to all believers, not just a handful of chosen ones. We shortchange the full gospel when we leave out any part—repentance, baptism in water, or baptism in the Holy Spirit. The Lord has given us all we need to be empowered disciples for His kingdom. The Holy Spirit is the Spirit of God Himself. He has given us His best—all of Him to impact all of me!

Why Should We Be Baptized in the Holy Spirit?
1. The Anointing—A Promise: Precious and Priceless

It means being filled with God. It is about real enablement, strength of character, healing and deliverance, protection, wisdom, favor, and goodness. We need Him to live this life.

I am going to send you what my Father has promised, but stay in the city until you have been clothed with power from on high (Luke 24:49).

And while staying with them he ordered them not to depart from Jerusalem, but to wait for the promise of the Father, which, he said, "You heard from me; For John baptized with water, but you will be baptized with the Holy Spirit not many days from now" (Acts 1:4-5).

He told them to wait for it. Jesus didn't start His ministry without the power of the Spirit, and He tells His disciples not to either. We are not to live our lives in our own strength and wisdom, but to call on the power He has made available to us.

For John truly baptized with water, but you shall be baptized with the Holy Spirit not many days from now (Acts 1:5 NKJV).

If you then, being evil, know how to give good gifts to your children, how much more you're your heavenly Father give the Holy Spirit to those who ask Him! (Luke 11:13 NKJV)

2. The Holy Spirit gave them power for witnessing and a supernatural life, and it is the power we still need today.

He is empowering us to be witnesses for Christ. The Spirit gives us power over sin, as well as our transformation to live, and speak, and act like Jesus. Speaking in tongues is evidence that the Holy Spirit is living in us—His presence is greater than all of the gifts! Praying in tongues proves there is nothing impossible with God. It is the perfect communication with God.

When the Day of Pentecost had fully come, they were all with one accord in one place. And suddenly there came a sound form heaven, as of a rushing mighty wind, and it filled the whole house where they were sitting. Then there appeared to them divided tongues, as of fire, and one sat upon each of them. And they were all filled with the Holy Spirit and began to speak with other tongues, as the Spirit gave them utterance (Acts 2:1-4 NKJV).

3. The Holy Spirit is our Helper, Teacher, and Comforter

We were never meant to do life on our own. God is saying that what He is promising us, His children—if we walk with Him—"It will not be by might, nor power, but *by My Spirit says the Lord of Hosts*" (Zechariah 4:6 NKJV). Don't let anything stop you from receiving this promise!

But the Helper, the Holy Spirit, whom the Father will send in my name, he will teach you all things and bring to your remembrance all that I have said to you (John 14:26).

4. Sign of the Presence and Power of the Holy Spirit

But I say, walk by the Spirit, and you will not gratify the desires of the flesh. For desires of the flesh are against the Spirit, and the desires of the Spirit are against the flesh, for these are opposed to each other, to keep you from doing the things you want to do. But if you are led by the Spirit, you are not under the Law. Now the works of the flesh are evident: sexual immorality, impurity, and sensuality; idolatry, sorcery, enmity, strife, jealousy, fits of anger, rivalries, dissensions, divisions, envy, drunkenness, orgies, and things like these. I warn you, as I warned you before, that those who do such things will not inherit the kingdom of God. But the fruit of the Spirit is love, joy, peace, patience, kindness, goodness, faithfulness, gentleness, self-control; against such things there is no law. And those who belong to Christ Jesus have crucified the flesh with its passions and desires. If we live by the Spirit, let us also keep in step with the Spirit. Let us not become conceited, provoking one another, envying one another (Galatians 5:16-26).

5. It was a Normal, Expected Experience
(Acts 2:38, Acts 10:44-46, 19:6, Ephesians 5:18)

While Peter was saying these things, the Holy Spirit fell on all those who heard the word (Acts 10:44).

Be filled with the Spirit (Ephesians 5:18).

Inspecting Your Foundation

The *fullness of the gospel foundation* (repentance, baptism in water, baptism in the Holy Spirit) should be every believer's normal Christian life. Reinhard Bonnke describes the baptism in the Holy Spirit as mortal man, quickened and made righteous, speaking in a heavenly language with His Father. What intimacy!

Who can be filled? How do you get baptized?
- The Baptism in the Spirit is for every disciple of Jesus (Acts 2:38-40).
- The Holy Spirit is not an "it"—but a Person.
- He is a GIFT from God. He can't be earned. He wants you to have HIM!
- The Holy Spirit is often received by laying hands on others but can be received on your own as well. Ask God and expect Him to fill you—begin praising Him and receive Him!
- If Jesus needed the power of the Spirit for His life and mission here on earth, how much more do we need it?
- Being filled with the Spirit is important to our Christian life. As we pray in the Spirit, we are praying the very will of God without our own agenda or flesh interfering.
- We continue to follow His command to be baptized with the Holy Spirit and receive power to live a holy life and power to be witnesses with boldness.

Don't Settle for Bondage—Fight and Believe!

God has a destiny for you as His child. The enemy's goal is to derail and thwart God's plan for your life. Jesus faced challenges just like us—that is why we have the Holy Spirit and can be covered by the full armor of God. Resist and stand against the enemy!

Put on the whole armor of God—the war against God's children is in full throttle, culturally, socially, morally, politically, physically, mentally, against religious freedoms and our families! When we don't fight, we are accepting everything as is and saying yes to the enemy, which allows him to reign and keep us in fear and bondage. Don't accept what the enemy is telling you—don't accept the counterfeit—don't settle for anything less than God, Himself!

God has set you free—Jesus has given us His inherent authority and power and instructions for life—to allow us to be victorious. Be courageous and stand firm in what God says! It is a good fight! The disciples fought against the Roman Empire to proclaim the Gospel, and they changed the world. Abraham fought a fight of faith. Joseph fought for hope instead of disappointment and rejection. David fought against feelings of doubt and all kinds of odds during a delay before he was crowned king.

Don't accept the enemy's attack on your walk with the Lord: your calling, your children, your marriage, your body, which is the temple of the Holy Spirit. Fight for it—be strong in the Lord and in the power of the Holy Spirit. Every challenge is a doorway to enter into your miracle, blessing, breakthrough, victory, and inheritance in Jesus' name! Every miracle proclaims that Jesus is alive!

Full Armor of God
Ephesians 6:10-20

Finally, my brethren, be strong in the Lord and in the power of His might. Put on the whole armor of God that you may be able to stand against the wiles of the devil. For we do not wrestle against flesh and blood, but against principalities, against powers, against the rules of the darkness of this age, against spiritual hosts of wickedness in the heavenly places. Therefore, take up the whole armor of God that you may be able to withstand the evil day, and having done all, to stand.

Stand therefore, having girded your waist with truth, having put on the breastplate of righteousness, and having shod your feet with the prepara-

tion of the gospel of peace; above all, taking the shield of faith with which you will be able to quench all the fiery darts of the wicked one.

And take the helmet of salvation, and the sword of the Spirit, which is the word of God; praying always with all prayer and supplication in the Spirit, being watchful to this end with all perseverance and supplication for all the saints—and for me, that utterance may be given to me, that I may open my mouth boldly to make known the mystery of the gospel, for which I am an ambassador in chains; that in it I may speak boldly, as I out to speak.

The armor of God is an amazing metaphor or action we need to take in our spiritual lives. Paul sets the scene—we are fighting a war, and the stakes are higher than they have ever been in human history. Our enemy? Not flesh and blood, no human foe. We fight against a much more fearsome opponent whose forces are described in Ephesians 6:12. Our adversary, Satan, the devil, and his host of demons have a single, driving purpose: obliterate the children of God.

We put on the armor of righteousness and receive strength from God to effectively wage war against our enemy. Without it we are helpless; but with it, we are soldiers for the living God and "more than conquerors through Him who loved us" (Romans 8:37)

It is up to you to trust and obey God for your life and your family. You have been given the armor of God because you have been appointed for nothing less than victory with a sound mind, healthy body, and renewed spirit.

Renew Your Mind on God's Word

These men who have turned the world upside down have come here also (Acts 17:6).

When this word of God was proclaimed, it agitated and stirred up the crowds.

The God who made the world and everything in it, being Lord of heaven and earth, doth not live in temples made by man, nor is he served by human hands, as though He needs anything, since He Himself gives all mankind life and breath and everything… Yet He is actually not far from each one of us, for in Him we live and move and have our being. The times of ignorance God overlooked, but now He commands all people everywhere to repent, because he has fixed a day on which he will judge the world in righteousness by a man he has appointed and of this he has given assurance to all by raising him from the dead…Some men mocked him and others joined him (Acts 17:24-25, 27, 30-32).

And I, when I came to you, brothers, did not come proclaiming to you the testimony of God with lofty speech or wisdom. For I decided to know nothing among you except Jesus Christ and him crucified. And I was with you in weakness and in fear and much trembling, and my speech and my message were not in plausible words of wisdom, but in demonstration of the Spirit and of power, so that your faith might not rest in the wisdom of men, but in the power of God.

Yet among the mature we do impart wisdom, although it is not a wisdom of this age or of the rules of this age, who are doomed to pass away. But we impart a secret and hidden wisdom of God, which God decreed before the ages for our glory. None of the rules of this age understood this, for if they had, they would not have crucified the Lord of glory. but, as it is written, "What no eye has seen, nor ear heard, nor the heart of man imagined, what God has prepared for those who love him, these things God has revealed to us through the Spirit. For the Spirit searches everything, even the depths of God. For who knows a person's thoughts except the spirit of that person which is in him? So also no one comprehends the thoughts of God except the Spirit of God.

Now we have received not the spirit of the world, but the Spirit who is from God, that we might understand the things freely given us by God. **And we impart this in words not taught by human wisdom but taught by the Spirit, interpreting spiritual truths to those who are spiritual. The natural person does not accept the things of the Spirit of God, for they are folly to him, and he is not able to understand** *them because they are spiritually discerned. The spiritual person judges all things, but is himself to be judged by no one. For who understood the mind of the Lord so as to instruct him? But **we have the mind of Christ*** (1 Corinthians 2:1-16).

Therefore, we are ambassadors for Christ, God making his appeal through us. We implore you on behalf of Christ, be reconciled to God For our sake he made him to be sin who knew no sin, so that in him we might become the righteousness of God (2 Corinthians 5:20-21).

Working together with him, then we appeal to you not to receive the grace of God in vain. ... behold now is the day of your salvation. You are not restricted by us, but you are restricted in your affections.

Do not be unequally yoked with unbelievers. For what partnership has righteousness with lawlessness? Or what fellowship has light with darkness? What accord has Christ with Belial? [A name given to Satan.] *Or what portion does a believer share with an unbeliever?*

What agreement has the temple of God with idols? *For we are the temple of the living God: as God said, "I will make my dwelling among them and walk among them, and I will be their God, and they shall be my people. Therefore, go out from their midst, and be separate from them, says the Lord, and touch no unclean thing; then I will welcome you, and I will be a father to you, and you shall be sons and daughters to me, says the Lord Almighty* (2 Corinthians 6:1-2, 12, 14-17)).

Since we have these promises, beloved, let us cleanse ourselves from every defilement of body and spirit, bringing holiness to completion in the fear of God (2 Corinthians 7:1).

Blessed is the man who remains steadfast under trial, for when he has stood the test he will receive the crown of life, which God has promised to those who love him. Let no one say when he is tempted, "I am being tempted by God, for God cannot be tempted with evil, and he himself tempts no one. But each person is tempted when he is lured and enticed by his own desire. Then desire when it has conceived gives birth to sin, and sin when it is fully grown brings forth death. Do not be deceived, my beloved brothers. Every good gift and every perfect gift is from above, coming down from the Father of lights, with whom there is no variation or shadow due to change. Of his own will he brought us forth by the word of truth, that we should be a kind of first fruits of his creatures (James 1:12-18).

But be doers of the word, and not hearers only, deceiving yourselves (James 1:22).

If anyone thinks he is religious and does not bridle his tongue but deceives his heart, this person's religion is worthless. Religion that is pure and undefiled before God the Father is this: to visit orphans and widows in their affliction, and to keep oneself unstained from the world (James 1:26-27).

Whoever says he abides in him ought to walk in the same way in which he walked (1 John 2:6).

Do not love the world for the things in the world. If anyone loves the world, the love of the Father is not in him. For all that is in the world—the desires of the flesh, and the desires of the eyes, and the pride of life—is not from the Father but is from the world. And the world is passing away along with it desires, but whoever does the will of God abides forever (1 John 2:15-17).

But the anointing that you received from him abides in you, and you have no need that anyone should teach you. But as his anointing teaches you about everything, and is true, and is no lie—just as it has taught you, abide in him (1 John 2:26).

The reason the Son of God appeared was to destroy the works of the devil (1 John 2:8b).

Beloved, if our heart does not condemn us, we have confidence before God; and whatever we ask we receive from him, because we keep his commandments and do what pleases him (1 John 3:21-22).

Whoever has the Son has life; whoever does not have the Son of God does not have life.

And this is the confidence that we have toward him, that if we ask anything according to his will he hears us. And if we know that he hears us in whatever we ask, we know that we have the request we have asked of him.

We know that everyone who has been born of God does not keep on sinning, but he who was born of God protects him, and the evil one does not touch him. We know that we are from God, and the whole world lies in the power of the evil one. And we know that the Son of God has come and has given us understanding, so that we may know him who is true; and we are in him who is true, in his Son, Jesus Christ, He is the true God and eternal life. Little children, keep yourselves from idols (1 John 5:12, 14-15, 18-20).

Beloved, I pray that all may go well with you and that you may be in good health, as it goes well with your soul. For I rejoiced greatly when the brothers came and testified to your truth, as indeed you are walking in the truth. I have no greater joy than to hear that my children are walking in the truth. (3 John 2-4).

Now to him who is able to keep you from stumbling and to present you blameless before the presence of his glory with great joy, 25 to the only God, our Savior, through Jesus Christ our Lord, be glory, majesty, dominion, and authority, before all time and now and forever. Amen (Jude 24-25).

So that we would not be outwitted by Satan; for we are not ignorant of his designs (2 Corinthians 2:11).

It happened that the father of Publius lay sick with fever and dysentery. And Paul visited him and prayed, and putting his hands on him, healed him. And when this had taken place, the rest of the people on the island who had diseases also come and were cured (Acts 28:8-9).

Peace, I Give To You

You will keep him in perfect peace, Whose mind is stayed on You, Because he trusts in You. Trust in the Lord forever, For in Yah, the Lord, is everlasting strength (Isaiah 26: 3-4 NKJV).

Perfect peace is expressed in Hebrew by a method of two words: *shalom, shalom*—putting emphasis on the word. According to scholars, the phrase *you will keep him in* implies everything: health, happiness, well-being, and peace. Because of Jesus, we now have His peace imparted to us. He reminds us of God's words when He gives us His peace with the new covenant.

Peace I leave with you. My peace I give to you; not as the world gives do I give to you. Let not your heart be troubled, neither let it be afraid (John 14:27 NKJV).

God continues to promise so many things as we love Him and walk in His ways. We are more than overcomers! We are victorious! We are loved and anointed! We are the righteousness of Christ and the temple of the Holy Spirit.

You have an anointing from the Holy One, and you know all things (2 John 2:20 NKJV).

But the anointing which you have received from Him abides in you, and you do not need that anyone teach you; but as the same anointing teaches you concerning all things, and is true, and is not a lie, and just as it has taught you, you will abide in Him (2 John 2:27 NKJV).

He who has My commandments, and keeps them, it is he who loves Me. And he who loves Me will be loved by My Father, and I will love him and manifest Myself to him (John 14:21 NKJV).

The word "manifest" (*Strong's* 1718), a Greek word meaning to cause to shine, thus to appear, reveal, exhibit, present oneself to the sight of another, and to declare and make known. Jesus completely aligned His life and will with His Father's. Jesus is saying that if we love Him, we will love His Father's Word also. Jesus desires to reveal Himself supernaturally as we love Him and make Him known. The world is desperately seeking hope and yet we are the carriers of Hope! We have a good news message, not in word only, but in the demonstration of God's love and power.

The things which you learned and received and heard and saw in me, these do, and the God of peace will be with you (Philippians 4:9 NKJV).

Go with renewed purpose and passion. Know with confidence that you are delivered from this evil world and are partakers of God's divine nature as you fulfill what God has called you to do. Recognize that you can't go by what you see or feel, but the Word of God is the standard. Use it as a way to see who you are in Christ. God has given you everything you need—Him! You are not alone.

I refused to be intimidated by a culture I've been called to impact. —*Bishop Tony Miller*

Live Loved; Live Well; Live Him!

God wants you well and fruitful. You *have been* delivered! God already dealt with the sin problem. He redeemed us from the curse so that we are rescued, healed, set free, and can walk in the fullness of God with Him! You can walk in a totally victorious life, but it all comes through renewing your mind by the word of God and in the knowledge of Him and all that He has given you. Know who you are—take your authority in Christ. Begin resisting (taking a stand against) the devil, and he will flee from you.

I am no longer an orphan or a victim. I have a new home in the Kingdom of God. I know so, because the King, my Dad, said so! I am defined by His promises and shaped by every word He says. He is all wisdom, provision, and wellness. Amazing grace! I was once blind, but now I can see. I was lame, but now I run. I was deaf, but now I hear Him call my name! I once was in bondage, but now I am free! Thank You, Jesus, how precious You are!

*Put a song in your heart as you pray Psalm 23—
make it personal! You are loved—live it!*

The LORD is my shepherd; I shall not want. He makes me to lie down in green pastures; He leads me beside the still waters. He restores my soul; He leads me in the paths of righteousness for His name's sake. Yea, though I walk through the valley of the shadow of death, I will fear no evil; For You are with me; Your rod and Your staff, they comfort me. You prepare a table before me in the presence of my enemies; You anoint my head with oil; My cup runs over. Surely goodness and mercy shall follow me All the days of my life; And I will dwell in the house of the LORD Forever (Psalm 23).

References

Ravenhill, D: *For God's Sake Listen: A prophetic word to the church,* 2013, Offspring Publishers.

Bonnke, R: *Holy Spirit: Are we flammable or fireproof?* Orlando, 2017, Christ For All Nations.

Koenig, H., King, C. and Carson, V: *The Handbook of Religion and Health,* 2012, Oxford University Press.

Donahue, MP: *Nursing the Finest Art: An illustrated history,* St. Louis, 1996, The CV Mosby Company.

Citizen's Commission on Human Rights (CCHR) website: http://www.cchr.org

Carl Jung Foundation Website: www.CarlJung.net

Bobgan, M. and Bobgan, D. (2012) *Psycho Heresy: The Psychological Seduction of Christianity.* Santa Barbara, CA: East Gate Publications.

Whitaker, R. (2005) *Anatomy of an Epidemic: Psychiatric Drugs and the Astonishing Rise of Mental Illness in America.* Ethical Human Psychology and Psychiatry, Volume 7, Number 1, 2005.

Stewart, D. (2012). *Healing Oils of the Bible.* Marble Hill, MO: Care Publications.

Olmsted, D. and Blaxill, M. (2017). *Denial: How refusing to face the facts about our autism epidemic hurts children, families, and our future.* New York: Skyhorse Publishers.

Heckenlively, K. and Mikovits, J. (2015/2017) *PLAGUE.* New York: Skyhorse Publishers.

Popoola, M. (2015) *Holistic and Complementary Therapies.* Brockton, MA: CE Express Western Schools.

Henley D, Lipson N, Korach K, Bloch C. *Prepubertal Gynecomastia Linked to Lavender and Tea Tree Oils.* New England Journal of Medicine, Feb. 1, 2007.

Brown, C. (2013). *The Healing Gods: Complementary and Alternative Medicine in Christian America.* New York: Oxford University Press.

About the Author

Jo McGuffin has an extensive background in healthcare education and administration. She is an ordained minister and Executive Director of Development, Zoe Healing Center. Zoe Healing Center is an organization comprised of multiple ministries of healing, equipping, and restoration of entire families.

Jo's passion for encouraging people to walk in the fullness of God's love and power for their lives is paramount in her life. Her messages of life and purpose are rallying a generation to embrace the broken-hearted and to become ambassadors of hope and healing through Jesus' finished work on the Cross.